D0498234

NUREYEV

Aspects of the Dancer

NUREYEV

Aspects of the Dancer

by JOHN PERCIVAL

G. P. PUTNAM'S SONS
NEW YORK

Drawing by Moira McCaffery, photographed by Cyril Williams. Photographs by Jane Brown; Louis van der Busken; Judy Cameron; Bob van Dantzig; Mike Davis; Fayer (Vienna); Beverly Gallegos; Mike Humphrey; Lido; Louis Peres; Terry Rowe (Australian Information Service); Enar Merkal Rydberg (Royal Theatre, Stockholm); Lesley E. Spatt; A. Traverso (Cannes); Rosemary Winckley

SBN: 399-11544-7
Library of Congress Catalog
Card Number: 75-21519

Contents

Illustrations are found following pages 96 and 160.

NU•RE•YEV (noŏ rā ef, -ev; *Russ.* noŏ Re' yef), *n.*
RUDOLF (HA•ME•TO•VICH)(hä me'to vich), born 1938,
Russian ballet dancer
 —*The Random House Dictionary*
 of the English Language

Introduction

EVERYBODY knows two things about Rudolf Nureyev: that he is a dancer and that he "leaped to freedom" when being sent back to the Soviet Union from Paris. The sensational circumstances of his arrival in the West brought instant fame, but that has proved a mixed blessing. When a man is so rarely out of the news, it is natural to suppose that his reputation is being built up by clever publicity, whereas the fact is that Nureyev does not bother to employ a press agent or any similar representative and is so chary of publicity that for a long time he even shunned interviews.

Before leaving the Soviet Union, he had already shown clearly enough that he did not need publicity to make his mark. He did not begin serious training as a dancer until well past the usual age, and when he began, his physique seemed so unsuitable that the other students laughed at him. In spite of that and in spite of a rebellious temperament that was always getting him into trouble with the authorities, he had succeeded not only in graduating into one of the most illustrious ballet companies in the world, but in being picked to start straightaway as a principal dancer, completely bypassing the usual process of entering the corps de ballet and working up through the ranks of soloists. He had even been chosen by the senior ballerina to partner her at his debut. Then, in only three seasons, he had begun to stamp his own interpretation on some of the most prized classical productions in the repertory. Amendments he had made to the interpretation of *La Bayadère* remain to this day in the Kirov production (although naturally without acknowledgment), and ideas which he had introduced into *Giselle* and *Swan Lake* have since won widespread acceptance. And he was still only twenty-three years old.

In the West, as well as being recognized as one of the greatest dancers of his day, Nureyev has become a star whose name is as familiar to the general public as it is to balletomanes. Yet in a sense his achievements have been only half realized. His fame as a dancer has overshadowed his other gifts, as a producer and a director, which I believe will eventually be seen to be equally outstanding.

I have tried in this book to do three things: to tell the story of his career so far, much more completely than has been done before; to describe his way of working, onstage and off; and to give my own assessment of his gifts and achievements. I thought it would also be interesting to gather comments and opinions from some of the dancers, choreographers and others who have worked with him. Their views will supplement my own and perhaps help kill the widespread myth that Nureyev is some kind of monster.

To me, he has been immensely helpful, especially in providing much unpublished information about his early years. For allowing me to draw upon his memory in many long conversations, to quote him on various subjects and to watch him in the unflattering conditions of class and rehearsal, I am grateful. He also made time to read the greater part of what follows in its early drafts and to make helpful suggestions and corrections. Any mistakes which remain are my own.

A Dancer's Life

RUDOLF Nureyev is able to explain briefly and specifically how he came to be a dancer. He told me, "There was simply from this quite early age the awareness that the only thing I wanted was to dance."

He was born on March 17, 1938, near Irkutsk, a city in the extreme south of the Soviet Union and nearer its eastern than its western limits, bordering on Mongolia. His father's artillery battalion had been stationed at Vladivostok, and the rest of the family, Rudolf's mother and three sisters, were traveling there to join him. The boy was actually born on the train as it traveled around Lake Baikal. That fact has often been seized upon, rather fancifully, as an omen of his future travels. More significantly, Nureyev has said that he never had the sense of belonging in one particular place or of a home or country to bind him to one spot. His mother (whom he resembles) and his eldest sister, Rosa, are very dear to him, but that is something quite different.

His parents were both Tartars. His mother came from the ancient city of Kazan on the Volga, his father from a village near Ufa, capital of the Bashkir Republic. The family name derives from an error by a recording official when the birth of Rudolf's father was registered. The grandfather's name was Nuri Fasli, and somehow the official heard only the first part of this, writing it down as Nureef. The y sound in the usual English version, Nureyev, simply represents the Russianized pronunciation of the Moslem suffix. Nuri's other son, Rudolf's uncle, still had the original family name.

Being a Tartar, Nureyev does not use the second name Hametovich ("son of Hamet") which Russian practice would give him. His surname is, of course, spelled differently in different countries to represent the same sound: Nouréev in France, Nurejew in Germany. However, even in France he spells his first name Rudolf, not Rudolph as it is often wrongly given in news stories.

In their youth, Nureyev's parents had been peasants, working on the land. The Russian Revolution had given them the chance of a better life for themselves and better prospects for their children. Naturally they became Communists, and the father, Hamet, joined the army as a political agent responsible for teaching other soldiers Russian history with special emphasis on the revolution and the achievements of the Communist Party.

The movements of his battalion made a nomadic life necessary for the family. When Rudolf was only a few months old, they moved to Moscow and spent the next three years there. When the Germans invaded in 1941, Hamet Nureyev became an ordinary soldier and was called away for war service. Soon afterward the house where the family lived in Moscow was hit by a bomb. They had to leave in a hurry but expected to return and left some of their possessions behind. Rudolf, then about three, remembers being pushed on a wheelbarrow with a kettle swinging from the back.

The mother and her four children were evacuated to a little village in the Bashkir Republic. Conditions in the Soviet Union were hard for everyone at that time, but especially for a family of forced evacuees. They had to share a room with another family, two very old Russians. That did at least have the advantage for the boy that the old couple gave him food, sweet potatoes or goat's cheese, as a reward for joining in their Christian prayers, although he neither understood nor believed what he was mumbling. In those days most people were hungry much of the time.

He was a lonely child and remembers no friends, no toys. The only person apart from his mother for whom he had great affection was his big sister Rosa, about ten years older than himself. When he hurt himself by pulling over the Primus stove on which the family's supper of potatoes was cooking, the fuss that was made of him in the hospital at Chelyabinsk became his first pleasurable memory, and the pictures of cows, with crayons for coloring them, which his mother brought him in the hospital, were the first possessions he had ever owned.

When he was five, the family moved to Ufa, which they had always considered their hometown. There they lived with his father's brother in what Nureyev described to me as a "crazy house." Like most of the buildings in Ufa at that time, it was built of wood. It had a steep roof forming a big loft, and it was only recently that talking about it, he came to wonder why none of them thought of making the loft habitable. The likeliest explanations he could think of were the difficulty of heating it and the even greater difficulty of getting official permission, since all houses were state-owned. As it was, the Nureyevs and two other families had to share a single room. Somehow they managed without getting too much on one another's nerves, but the conditions must have been appalling. Incidentally, the house no longer exists; not long ago Nureyev saw a photograph of a big block of flats on the same site.

Ufa lies on the eastern side of the Ural Mountains. The climate is hot in summer, bitterly cold in winter. Fuel was short as well as food; life was cold and dark and bleak. The family sold or exchanged everything they could for food, even Hamet's civilian clothes. When the time came for Rudolf, at six, to enter the infants' school, he had no shoes, and for a coat he had to wear his sister Lida's cape. Not surprisingly, the other children made fun of him, but he took it quietly, probably withdrawing further into himself and his habitual loneliness. Although wartime shortages affected everyone, children from long-established local families were not so hard hit as the family who had fled from Moscow, leaving most of their possessions behind.

Nureyev tells the story of how his mother was nearly killed by wolves, walking home from a village thirty kilometers away (nearly twenty miles in each direction) where she had gone on foot to visit relatives who could supply a few potatoes. That gives the measure of the plight the family was in during the war. It is not surprising that he does not like dwelling on that time, and it would be purely speculative to wonder whether those privations might have helped at all to build up in him the extraordinary drive and determination which have fueled his career.

On the other hand, one can certainly see in the lonely child the beginnings of the self-sufficiency which is part of his genius. Poor, hungry and alone he may have been, but he does not give the impression of having been a pathetic figure. He took pleasure in listening to music on the radio and in watching the people in the streets going about their everyday affairs, which he often found funny, especially the men in their pajamas or bathrobes hurrying to the steam baths on a Sunday. He particularly enjoyed watching trains gradually gather speed as they left Ufa station, a splendid marble building, intended to give a fine impression of the town to anyone passing through.

When he was seven, Rudolf transferred from the infants' school to what he described as "real school," and at once he loved it. He had a capacity to grasp everything the first time he was told it, and this quickly put him at the top of his class. There soon came an added pleasure when the class was taught to sing and dance simple Bashkir songs. From the way he describes it, the impression is that the music was what first filled him with an almost delirious joy, but it was his dancing that impressed other people. He would sing and dance all the time when he came home from school until it was time to go to bed. His enthusiasm was reinforced when the school sent groups of children to perform in hospitals for wounded soldiers back from the war. He enjoyed these concerts, looked forward to them and found dancing becoming more precious to him all the time.

On New Year's Eve in that first year at the real school, when he was still under eight years of age, Nureyev made up his mind that he was going to be a dancer. That night there was a gala ballet performance in Ufa. The city today has more than half a million inhabitants. It has been growing steadily since before the Revolution, and although the sharpest increase did not come until the development of the Baku oilfields after the war, it was already an important regional center. Its principal lyric theater is called the Bashkir Opera and Ballet Theater. Although virtually unknown in the West, its ballet ranks moderately high among the three dozen or so permanent professional companies in the Soviet Union. It was in Ufa, incidentally, that Fedor Chaliapin began his career, a fact I learned only when Nureyev happened to mention it, since it is not given in any of the reference books I have looked at. If they give any account at all of Chaliapin's earliest appearances, the location is specified only in some such phrase as "a provincial opera house." There is a nice irony in the thought of that disparaged theater in Ufa having provided the first stage for so great a singer and later for such a great dancer, too.

Nureyev's mother had managed to buy just one ticket for the ballet that night, but the whole family was determined to squeeze in somehow. That is not so difficult a process as it must sound to most readers. I have known, for instance, of people who managed to get into sold-out London theaters without a ticket if they were determined enough. On that occasion in Ufa in 1945 the process was helped by the presence outside the theater of an excited crush of people who pushed forward and broke the doors open. In the confusion, mother, three daughters and son all slipped through.

The theater made an enormous impression on the boy, who was struck with wonder at the chandeliers, the glowing lamps, the colored glass windows, the velvet and gold. But the ballet itself impressed him even more. It was *The Song of the Cranes,* based on a Bashkir legend of good triumphing over evil. A girl and a shepherd, representing innocence, defeated the plots of a cruel, cunning rich man to possess the girl. The first specifically Bashkir ballet, it had been created during the war with music by two composers, Lev Stepanov and Z. Ismagilov, and choreography by Nina Anisimova.

The leading role was danced by the ballerina Zaituna Nazretdinova, who was very highly regarded. Even looking back with more mature judgment, Nureyev still thinks her a beautiful dancer. At that time he was enraptured by the whole experience. After that night he had just one ambition. Perhaps ambition is not strong enough to describe his feelings: he was determined to dance. How to achieve that intention was another matter.

People who saw him dancing kept saying how good he was and suggesting that he should be sent to Leningrad to study. But Leningrad was 1,700 kilometers away, more than 1,000 miles; in the family's circumstances at that time, they might just as well have said send him to the moon. The idea of studying in that famous school became a dream, an obsession.

Meanwhile, he continued dancing in the school groups. They competed against other schools and won. Sometimes they gave public concerts. At the age of ten all the children had to join the Pioneers, where their activities were rather like the Scouts but also included learning folk dances from many other regions of the Soviet Union, which one of the Pioneer leaders taught them from a magazine. That very much enlarged their repertory.

However, young Nureyev's enthusiasm for dancing was doing him no good at all as far as his schoolteachers were concerned. All his energy went into that one activity, and from being good at all other subjects he declined drastically. The only person to understand and encourage his eager ambition was his sister Rosa. She was studying to be a teacher, and her course included music and some dancing. She told her young brother about the history of the dance, took him with her to some lectures, sometimes brought home costumes for him to look at. He would gaze, stroking and smoothing and smelling them like the addict he had become.

It was not until he was eleven that Nureyev had his first ballet lessons. He was taken by one of the Pioneer mistresses to the Ufa Scientists' Club to meet an old lady named Udeltsova, then about seventy, who had been a member of Serge Diaghilev's corps de ballet. She still taught, not professional students but children. Nureyev was made to dance for her: a gopak, a lezginka and other folk dances. As he danced, the old lady looked stunned, and at the end she gave him the advice he had already heard from others: "Go to Leningrad, study there." But from her lips it meant something at last, and the boy blushed. Besides, she was much more peremptory: "Child, you have a duty to yourself to learn classical dancing." Also, she could do something to help.

For the next year, Udeltsova gave Nureyev ballet classes twice a week. He began to learn the rudiments: the five standard positions of the feet, pliés, battements. And she taught him far more than basic technique. She was a cultured woman, had seen the best of Russian dancing and exotic dancers too, Japanese and Indian; she still went every year to Leningrad to keep in touch with what was happening. She told her young pupils about what she had seen, and for Nureyev it was a revelation. In particular, he was struck by what she said about Anna Pavlova, how that great dancer concealed the mechanics of her art and used her highly developed technique to give an illusion of spontaneity. From that he took his own aim as a dancer.

After a year Udeltsova passed Nureyev on to another teacher, a professional this time, named Vaitovich, who had been a soloist at the Kirov Ballet in Leningrad before returning to Ufa to teach. Vaitovich had the ability to jump higher than most dancers, and she was able to transmit that ability to her eager pupil. A really high jump is the most spectacular of assets for a male dancer, but it is rare. Even Vakhtang Chabukiani, the almost legendary leading man of Soviet ballet during the three decades from 1930, according to Nureyev did not really go high, at least in later years, but gave an illusion of lightness by the seeming ease and perfection with which he leaped.

Under his new teacher, Nureyev was making progress. Then came the news that a group of children from the whole Bashkir Republic was to be selected and sent to Leningrad to audition for entry to the Vaganova School associated with the Kirov Theater there. By that time Hamet Nureyev was back from the war. Rudolf, who had no earlier memories of him, found his father a stern, almost frightening man but pestered him to find out how the group was being selected, so as to apply for inclusion. Hamet was none too pleased to find that his only son had grown up to be interested only in something as "unmanly" as dancing and told the boy to forget the whole thing. Eventually he yielded to the boy's entreaties sufficiently to make a tentative inquiry from the cashier at the opera house. There they received the news that the party had already left. For the boy who thought that his great chance had come, this disappointment was a time of complete despair.

To make matters worse, his parents now forbade Nureyev to continue dancing. They had big ambitions for him: to study and become a doctor or an engineer perhaps. Nobody in the family had previously had the chance of higher education, and they could not understand how he could fail to be as keen about getting it as they were on his behalf. Since they had struggled for the Revolution and all the benefits it had brought to ordinary people, it must have been a bitter blow for them to see a child of theirs completely without ambition—which was the way it appeared to them. Dancing, what kind of career was that? In his father's view, it was fit only for idlers, and that was what Rudolf would become if he took it up. He should concentrate on his schoolwork, do well in his examinations, qualify for further studies, make something of his life. But if he really would not do those things, then the best thing was to start earning some money as soon as possible (he was now about fourteen) instead of all this nonsense.

To carry on with his dancing lessons or rehearsals in those circumstances necessitated a series of tricks and lies. He would offer to go out for the shopping, for instance, and return very late. Once he even managed to lose all the ration coupons for a week and was terrified.

His only ally, Rosa, had gone to Leningrad, but luckily he acquired another, the lady who played the piano for the Pioneers' dancing classes. When he was about fifteen, still hoping that his chance would come, still determined to try but not believing that it could really succeed, she got him the chance to walk on at the Ufa Opera House. It was not very glorious, playing a page or a beggar or carrying a spear as a Roman soldier, but it earned him ten rubles a night.

Unfortunately it involved missing lessons at school to attend rehearsals, making life even more complicated and exacerbating the bad reports he was already receiving from his teachers. The crisis was serious enough to give him the nerve to go to various workers' collectives, announce himself grandly as "an artist from the Ufa Opera" and offer to give them weekly lessons in folk dancing for 200 rubles a month. What they thought of the cheek of that skinny fifteen-year-old, I shudder to think, and probably he does too in retrospect, but he was convincing enough for them to give him a chance. In that way he found himself earning, with the money as an extra at the theater too, as much as his father was receiving at the time. That stopped the complaints at home for a while.

Meanwhile, the pianist who had secured the walk-on job

for him was trying to organize some even more valuable help. She gathered signatures from prominent local citizens on letters which she dispatched to the Ministry of Culture in Moscow, urging them to consider this talented boy for a scholarship to the Kirov School and assuring them how worthy of it he was. It is a pity that the good citizens who supported the request never had the chance to see onstage the outcome of their efforts, but a friend of Nureyev's who visited Ufa not long ago did at least discover that he is still remembered there as a local folk hero.

In his last year at school, just before the final examinations, he was offered the chance actually to dance at the opera house in a ballet called *Polish Ball*. After his years of folk dancing with school and Pioneer groups, in all sorts of unfavorable circumstances, sometimes even on a fitted-up stage on the back of a truck, he was actually taking part in a real performance in a real theater. The excitement was so much that he lay awake the whole night afterward. What role did you play? I asked him, thinking that the ballet must have had a child character in it, but he replied, "It was just in the corps de ballet, not really a role at all." That is the measure of how stagestruck he was, to be kept awake by that.

Immediately afterward he took his school examinations. He was sure he had failed, and he was right. Much more important, however, so far as he was concerned, was an offer to go on a month's tour through Bashkir with the Ufa Opera. He was still only walking on but earning money regularly, and he saved enough to buy himself a rail ticket to Moscow. There he spent three days walking through the city, all day and most of the night, too. He lived cheaply, sleeping (like so many students who are hard up) where he could, on a bench or in a station waiting room. It was his first experience of a great city, and from the way he takes in everything wherever he goes, it is easy to imagine the way he must have observed the crowds and the buildings, building his own impression of what would face him when he achieved his ambition to leave Ufa.

Back home, he was taken on as an apprentice member of the corps de ballet in spite of his lack of anything more than the bare minimum of training. His fanatical enthusiasm and his unusual quickness in grasping anything new enabled him to get by, and at the same time he had the chance at last to take regular classes with professional dancers. That was vital, because he now heard that he would be allowed to audition for a scholarship at Leningrad the following year, and he could not expect to be taken on so much past the normal starting age (nine or ten) without a fairly substantial grounding in classical technique.

Luckily, the Ufa company was not at all what would be found in any other country in a comparatively modest provincial capital. Throughout the Russian republics there is a real love of art which had been carefully fostered. Since the 1930s a measure of priority had been given to building up orchestras, drama, opera and ballet in all the different regions. The Ufa Ballet, which already drew most of its soloists from the Leningrad school, had benefited further during the war when some dancers from the Kirov Ballet (which naturally took the pick of the Leningrad graduates) were evacuated there and stayed on. When Nureyev, on his arrival in the West, first danced with the International Ballet of the Marquis de Cuevas, a company which for some years had toured successfully throughout Europe, he compared its general standard unfavorably with what he had known in Ufa. Also, Ufa was lucky in having an outstanding ballerina to head the company. Nureyev told me, "Nazretdinova had been a pupil of Vaganova, I think." Vaganova was the outstanding postrevolutionary teacher in Leningrad. "She was one of the first dancers after Ulanova to be given the title People's Artist of the USSR. Of course she was not like Ulanova, but she was a very good dancer."

The repertory was based on the old classics, not only *Swan Lake* but others, less widely performed, like *Esmeralda* and *Raymonda,* together with some of the standard Soviet productions such as *The Fountain of Bakhchisarai* and a few works specially created for the company. Although he was only an aspirant member, the experience would be useful, and Nureyev did not just experience it passively. His own description of that year is that "I worked like a madman." That did not prevent several reports of bad behavior and indiscipline being made against him. Even at that age, his eagerness to get on obviously did not make him at all compliant with conventional ways or rigid rules. Nevertheless, his ability was clear enough for the director to offer him, at the end of the year, a contract to stay as a full member of the company instead of going off to Leningrad. It was a compliment, but luckily for all of us, the thought of the Kirov was by now so firmly fixed in his mind that he turned down the offer.

He got two-thirds of the way there—as far as Moscow—with the Ufa company. A special festival called a "Decade of Bashkir Art" was being organized for presentation in Moscow during late May and early June, 1955. These "decades" were ten-day seasons designed to show the contribution to the arts of a specific region, with ballets, operas and plays. The Ufa Ballet proposed to present *Laurencia* and *The Song of the Cranes,* and the commissioner responsible for the arrangements came to see and approve these. Then one of those situations arose which are so frequent in plays and films that they sound slightly spurious when they happen in real life. A soloist who should have danced in *The Song of the Cranes* failed to arrive for the audition. For some reason, no understudy was available, and the director asked whether any of the other dancers would volunteer to take over. Nureyev had never learned that solo, but gambling on his exceptional memory for any dance he had seen, he put his hand up.

There was time for the ballet master to go through it with him hurriedly, and then he was onstage. He told me, "I had just about five minutes to prepare for that. It was a character dance. Bashkir dancing is full of big jumps, and also stamping, something like in Spanish dancing, so there are problems of timing. Luckily I had a good memory and managed to bring it off." But if it was memory and natural flair that got him through the steps, he thinks too that the ardor and sincerity of his feelings must have communicated themselves to the watchers and given his performance an emotional conviction.

There could be no leaving him out of the Moscow trip now, but after they arrived, there was another calamity. An intense schedule of rehearsals was started (three on the day of arrival), and Nureyev, as a very junior member of the company, was not used to this. Also, he was excited and perhaps overtired. Whatever the cause, he landed heavily and hurt his toes, causing his foot to swell up alarmingly. Performance, rehearsal, class, audition—they all were impossible in that state, and he had visions of once more losing the hopes that had seemed so near realization. But after a week his toes had healed, and on the advice of the rehearsal pianist who had already done so much to help him, Nureyev went along to the Bolshoi Theater, where Asaf Messerer was giving class.

One of the greatest dancers of his generation, Messerer (who, at fifty-one, retired only that year from the stage) is also an outstanding teacher, whose class is attended by leading members of the Bolshoi Ballet. Attending it must have been a formidable experience for the youngster. Later in his career, it was to be in Messerer's classroom that Nureyev met Galina Ulanova, whom he found to be "a very warm person." That came about because he was visiting Moscow, went to the Bolshoi to study, and when he entered the classroom some of the other dancers, as a practical joke, "told me to stand in the place which, though I did not know it, was where she always stood. When she arrived, she did not say anything, but she went up and down and kind of hovered by me, so I moved aside, but she told me to stay there. Messerer's class was very complicated because he choreographed it all the time, and she helped me by explaining everything."

However, that was all in the future. On this first visit he had less luck. Things started well, with Messerer agreeing to audition the boy when class ended, but he was unexpectedly called away before the end and, although Nureyev waited, did not return.

The next day, when Nureyev again turned up, he learned that Messerer had actually been called away from Moscow, but this time another teacher agreed to examine him. The result was even better than Nureyev could possibly have hoped for. He was told that if he entered the Bolshoi School, he would probably be allowed to join the eighth grade, only one grade down from the highest, and as far as he could have reached by that age if he had worked his way up from the normal age of entry.

That was a real temptation, but against it had to be set the disadvantage that the Moscow school was not residential, so if he went there, he would be expected to find his own lodgings and food, and he had no idea how he might get a scholarship, if at all. So off he went to Leningrad, buying only a single ticket and being so eager to get there that he did not even read the railway timetable carefully enough and got on an economy train that took twice as long on the journey as other trains (sixteen hours instead of eight) and was so full that he had to spend the whole time in the corridor.

As the train approached his dream city, the boy saw heavy, smoky clouds hanging over the suburbs with their factory chimneys and, being unused to this, thought they were running into a storm. So he first stepped into the streets of Leningrad wrapped in his big raincoat, only to find himself in bright sunshine. Like another famous dancer, Marius Petipa, who had made a similar arrival a century earlier, he did not let his unsuitable attire depress him but hurried straight to the Theater School in Rossi Street. Here, again like Petipa, he was told that he had arrived too soon and should return in a week's time when the holiday ended. The person he spoke to was no less a man than the school's director, Chelkov, who treated the brusque young stranger kindly enough at that first meeting, although later they got on less well.

Udeltsova, Nureyev's first teacher and patron, was in Leningrad at the time, and the boy went to stay with her at the home of her daughter, who was a psychiatrist. He spent his unexpected holiday exploring the city on foot from morning to night, finding himself at once responding to its buildings and prospects, its light and its inhabitants, its history and its traditions.

Nowhere were those traditions stronger than at the Leningrad State Academic Vaganova Choreographic Institute, to give the famous school its full official title. It was the direct descendant of the dancing school authorized by the Empress Anna Ivanovna in a decree dated May 4, 1738. Most of the best Russian dancers from that day to this studied there, including such world-famous stars as Nijinsky, Pavlova and Ulanova. The actual system of teaching had been overhauled in Soviet times, notably by the distinguished teacher Agrippina Vaganova, from whom the school now takes its name, but her changes were designed to develop and enhance the classical technique of previous generations, not to overthrow it. Similarly, the ideological basis of the teaching had altered since czarist days; the boys, for instance, no longer wore military-style uniforms. But one form of control had merely been replaced by another. Discipline now was enforced through the party machinery, and indoctrination to serve the state continued in its revised form as strictly as ever. For Nureyev the enthusiast, the school offered the finest teaching available anywhere in the world, which he was avid to accept, but Nureyev the individualist soon clashed with the rules and conventions of the organization.

His entrance examination took place on August 24, 1955, and was conducted by an outstanding teacher named Costravitskaya. Nureyev was examined together with a group of Latvians. At the end, Costravitskaya walked up to him and said, "Young man, you'll become either a brilliant dancer or a total failure—and most likely you'll be a failure." He had the sense to interpret this as a challenge to acquire the knowledge, control and understanding which would allow his natural talent to express itself properly, without letting his spontaneity and individuality be lost.

Nobody could doubt his quality, but at an age when some dancers already have a fully developed professional technique, he was still raw and hardly trained at all.

The new term began on September 1, so Nureyev had several days to get used to the building, where he slept in a dormitory with nineteen other students and ate in the canteen, three meals a day. Once work started, the classes could begin as early as eight in the morning and go on until seven in the evening. Two hours of classical dance and two of character dancing formed part of the daily schedule. In addition, there were classes in the history of art, ballet and music, which Nureyev enjoyed, and other academic subjects which, with his one overwhelming interest and aim in life, bored him and seemed a waste of precious time.

Chelkov, the director, decided to start Nureyev in the sixth grade, which he taught himself. That upset the young dancer in two respects. After what he had been told at the Bolshoi School in Moscow, he had expected to start higher, and now he realized that he might be called up for military service before he could complete the course; such an interruption would probably ruin his chances. Once accepted in the company, he would be exempt. Also, he found that Chelkov kept picking on him in what he thought an unfair way and humiliating him in front of everybody. It is possible that this was Chelkov's way of trying to provoke the boy into working hard: if so, he had misjudged his pupil's temperament. Possibly, however, Chelkov privately disagreed with Costravitskaya's decision to admit Nureyev and was more conscious of his faults than his promise. Whatever the motive, it put Nureyev into a rebellious mood.

That mood was soon reinforced by logic. Since he was intending to become a dancer, it seemed sensible to Nureyev that he should see as much ballet as possible. Consequently, after about a week, he deliberately defied the rule which forbade students to go out at night and went to the Kirov Theater to see a performance of *Taras Bulba*.

Retribution was immediate. He arrived back in the dormitory to find that his bed and his meal tickets had been removed in his absence. He spent the night on the floor, without sleeping much, went to class the next morning without breakfast, and fainted. When he came to, he told the teacher that he could not have been treated worse in the days of Alexander I, then walked out to get some food and sleep. For this, he found himself reported to Chelkov, who demanded to know who his friends in Leningrad were and even snatched his address book from him, thus increasing Nureyev's sense of injustice.

A week later he was back in Chelkov's office, having summoned up courage to explain his anxiety about not having time to complete the course unless allowed to transfer to the eighth grade. Chelkov was apparently astonished at such a demand but agreed to it, warning Nureyev that he had only himself to blame if his new teacher, Alexander Pushkin, refused to waste any time on him. Later, when Pushkin had become like a second father to Nureyev, he told him that Chelkov had announced that he was sending "an obstinate little idiot" to join his class and that if Pushkin agreed with his own assessment of the boy, they would have to expel him.

At first, Pushkin did in fact ignore Nureyev in class, as Chelkov had warned. In spite of that, Nureyev realized that he was now with a really exceptional teacher and worked harder than ever. The other eight students in the class had no time for him at all. They all had worked their way up through the school and naturally had achieved a higher standard of technique than his. He told me, "They held me and forced me to look at myself in the mirror. 'What kind of dancer do you think you are?' they asked me. They laughed at me, and of course my untrained muscles could not compare with theirs." But that kind of criticism did not worry him in the way Chelkov's sarcasm had done. It was something that he could see to be at least partly justified and something he could fight against, too. His response was to spend hours practicing on his own, repeating again and again the things he knew he was weakest in. "Because I started late, I had to work harder. Cabrioles, for instance, I did not find easy, so I did them over and over, jumping straight toward the mirror so that the faults showed. I could have done them sideways and looked good without so much trouble, but then I would not have got it right."

During that first year he made better progress than anyone, except perhaps himself, could have foreseen. At the end of the year each pupil was expected to perform a solo during the examinations held on the stage of the Kirov Theater, but Pushkin decided it was too soon for Nureyev to take part. So Nureyev started to work in secret on the man's solo from the *Diana and Acteon* pas de deux, a showpiece that contained some prodigious jumps. Nureyev's ability to absorb a role quickly enabled him to learn it, and he spent hours rehearsing on his own until he decided that he had mastered it sufficiently to show Pushkin. Then he asked his teacher to watch him in it and on the strength of that was allowed to take part in the end-of-year examination after all. One of the other pupils was entering the same solo, which added an element of competition, spurring Nureyev on. Afterward nobody congratulated him, but nobody made fun of him either, which he took as justification of his effort. He was now accepted.

But in another sense he refused to be accepted. He had

28

joined the Pioneers because it was compulsory. There was no such obligation to join the Komsomol, the organization for a higher age range of young people, but membership was expected all the same. Although the son of two party members, Nureyev had never had any interest in politics, and he had an objection to the kind of group activity and communal self-criticism which membership involved. The only kind of self-criticism he wanted was the genuine kind, and his instinct for privacy was a strong motive against joining. So he refused and inevitably became an object of suspicion. As he had by now made some friends outside the school, people who shared his interests, especially in music, he was regarded as a dangerous individualist. This was exacerbated by his habit of going most nights to a concert or ballet performance, sometimes even flying off to Moscow to see a special performance there.

At work, however, he had no further trouble. Pushkin's great virtue as a teacher, apart from the skill and experience he shared with the other members of the Leningrad staff, was his capacity to see each pupil's merits and understand how to get the best out of him. The way he saw into the nature of his pupils, encouraging each one and devising ways to help him, appealed especially to Nureyev, who wanted to keep the inner conviction which had first made him a dancer. His second year of studies with Pushkin went well, and at the end of it Pushkin proposed that Nureyev should spend a further year at the school, repeating the curriculum of the ninth (top) grade so as to consolidate and extend the progress he had made. That extra year had another advantage which was to become apparent only later. As Nureyev put it, "In the school, each class gives a concert three times a year in the small theater, before an audience of teachers and other students, and in class we study all the variations from the standard repertory. Those years with Pushkin were the time when I learned all the repertory." Among the roles he performed at the school concerts were the pas de deux from Fokine's *Chopiniana* (or *Les Sylphides,* as it is known in the West), from the second act of *Giselle* and from Acts 2 and 3 of *Swan Lake.* He also danced the solo of the romantic hero Vaczlav from *The Fountain of Bakhchisarai* and took part in a pas de quatre staged by Pushkin. At this time, too, he learned other roles which he did not dance publicly until years later.

During Nureyev's final year at the school the main company of the Kirov Ballet went on a tour to Eastern Europe. In their absence, performances were given at the Kirov Theater by a certain number of dancers who had remained behind, reinforced by senior students. At those performances Nureyev danced nine times as the Prince in *The Nutcracker,* partnering his fellow student Alla Sizova, and four times in the pas de trois in *Swan Lake* with two other youngsters, Galina Ivanova and Nina Yastrebova.

In June, 1958, a national competition for young ballet dancers was held in Moscow, and Nureyev entered it, dancing three contrasted pieces, all calling for virtuosity. One of them was the *Diana and Acteon* duet, the solo from which had already proved so auspicious for him. Although *Diana and Acteon* nowadays is generally given on its own as a concert piece, it comes from the old ballet *Esmeralda,* which had been revived at the Kirov in 1935 by Vaganova. Various changes were made at that time, but Nureyev tells me that Kirov tradition had it that the pas de deux at least was authentically old, probably close to the original choreography by Jules Perrot, who created the ballet in London (1844) and mounted it in St. Petersburg (now Leningrad) five years later. Acteon's solo, however, had been reworked by Vakhtang Chabukiani in 1935 to show off his own bravura technique. Chabukiani had done the same for the man's solo in the pas de deux from *The Corsair*, which was another of Nureyev's choices for the Moscow competition and has since become one of the works most closely associated with him. His partner in both those works was again Sizova. Nureyev's other entry was a solo from *Gayane*, the one in which the dancer carries a torch in each hand while he dances.

The evening was a great success for Nureyev, and he even had to repeat part of *The Corsair* because of the applause. When I asked him who had won what, he told me, "I don't think there were any prizes, I don't remember any, but I was pleased that they singled me out among the Leningrad dancers, and I was the only dancer from the Leningrad school to be chosen for the film they made. I think they rather tried to push Sizova down. Maximova was praised with Vassiliev, and Riabinkina—she had a wonderful fresh quality then—and Makarova was there already, dancing with Soloviev." What pleased Nureyev especially was that not only had his dancing delighted the audience and been admired by Vladimir Vassiliev, the best of the Moscow graduates that year, but this deliberate choice of such contrasted parts had been noticed and commended. He was happy, too, that his beloved teacher Pushkin shared in the credit.

The film about Russian ballet, in which Nureyev's *Corsair* solo was included as a result of that competition, had an interesting aftermath, since it must have been that which David Blair saw a while later and was so impressed that he persuaded Frederick Ashton to include some of the same sequences of steps in his main solo as Colas in *La Fille mal gardée*, so that Nureyev's influence indirectly en-

31

tered the Royal Ballet a couple of years before he first danced with them.

Another consequence of the competition was that two Moscow companies, the Bolshoi and the Stanislavsky, both offered Nureyev contracts as a leading dancer. The Bolshoi offer was a real temptation, but back in Leningrad (where he again had an exhilarating success in his final examinations, dancing a similar group of contrasted items) it was matched by an equal offer from the Kirov when Natalia Dudinskaya invited him to partner her. Dudinskaya was the senior ballerina and wife of the company's director and leading man, Konstantin Sergeyev, so to be picked to dance with her was an honor. There were other factors weighting the balance in favor of the Kirov besides the proud traditions of the company, although Nureyev was conscious of those and of his own links with the school. There was also the fact that he felt an atmosphere of greater artistic freedom in Leningrad than in Moscow, where the ballet was so much a showplace for tourists and official visitors. So the Kirov it was, and he was so keen to start work that instead of going on vacation when the school broke up, he stayed the few extra weeks until the company's season ended in August.

After that, his only thought was complete rest, but on vacation in the Crimea he received a telegram informing him that to repay his debt to Bashkir, since part of his scholarship had come from local funds, he was officially allocated to the Ufa Ballet. Whether this was just officialdom gone wrong or, as he suspected, a trick by his enemies, we are never likely to know. He flew at once to Moscow, where a woman at the Ministry of Culture (which is responsible, directly or indirectly, for the finances of all artistic enterprises throughout the USSR) refused to budge from what the telegram had said. Panicking, Nureyev tried to pull strings to get his offer to join the Bolshoi renewed. But on going back to Leningrad to collect his possessions, he was told by the Kirov Theater director to stay there and not be silly. He took the advice and heard nothing further about transfer to Ufa, but he was conscious that by renewing and then once more abandoning the idea of going to the Bolshoi, he had probably again upset people.

Nureyev's debut as a full member of the Kirov Ballet was in *Laurencia,* a ballet with choreography by Chabukiani based on Lope de Vega's play *Fuente Ovejuna.* It is about a revolt in fifteenth-century Spain against a tyrannical local lord. Dudinskaya played the role, which had been created for her, of the heroine whose rage, after the Comendador has exercised his *droit du seigneur* on her wedding day, drives the villagers to their insurrection. Nureyev took Chabukiani's own former role as her fiancé, Frondoso. The brilliant classical pas de six which he has since mounted for the Royal Ballet forms part of their wedding celebration and contrasts with the violent drama and free style of movement which follow in the course of the full work.

The ballet needs both virtuosity and a strong sense of character from its leading dancers. The reason why Nureyev was given the opportunity to dance it so young is that there was no other man in the company at the time who could manage it, and Dudinskaya was naturally glad of the chance to appear again in one of her most famous roles. Fortunately, Nureyev was not overawed at having to dance his graduation performance with the prima ballerina: "It was very flattering to be asked to do this role with her, and while we were dancing, I was conscious only of the character she was playing, so the question of age did not arise."

But before the second scheduled performance Nureyev

suffered a serious accident. He had been working on his own all day at the many solos. When the time came in the evening for an officially scheduled rehearsal, he was already exhausted, but a company coach made him continue and he tore a ligament. He was rushed to a hospital, where a doctor forecast that it would be two years before he could dance again. In that time his muscles would have lost all their newly acquired skill and strength, and his career might well have been finished. But thanks to loving care from Pushkin and his wife, who took him into their own home, he was back on his feet after three weeks and working again after another three. I suspect, from his response to later injuries, that in fact he was then by no means fit but simply determined that pain was not going to stop him from succeeding.

He recovered in time to take part in the International Youth Festival held in Vienna in 1959, but only after he had protested because his name was not on the first list of the Russian contingent (already his nonmembership in the "collective" was having an effect). Rehearsals for the competition were held in Moscow, where the Kirov contingent found a fencing club to work in. This had no barre for the warming-up exercises which begin every ballet class, no mirrors for the dancers to see their faults and correct them, not even a suitable floor for dancing. The conditions will sound horribly familiar to every dancer who has toured in British provincial towns, but they are not what ought to be expected, least of all when dancers from a major company are preparing to represent their country abroad. The other members of the Kirov group were ready to accept the arrangements, however, without protest, but Nureyev said it was impossible. That led to an argument with the teacher in charge, which ranged widely enough for Nureyev to express his belief that Soviet ballet was stressing technique at the expense of individual talent and that conformity would be the death of art. This speech was received in silence.

Although in disfavor because of this incident, Nureyev went with the others, who included his partner Sizova, Irina Kolpakova and Yuri Soloviev from Leningrad, Ekaterina Maximova and Vladimir Vassiliev from Moscow, all future stars, as well as other promising dancers whose careers were less sustained. After he had danced, he said, "They told me I had won first prize, and then a little later I heard someone else had been given it. In the end all our group were given first prizes, and then the dancers from the satellite countries also, so everybody won." So much for individuality! Nureyev worked off his feelings by telling a slightly coarse joke about two chickens, which summed up his view of the incident in a humorous and laconic way, but of course, he found himself in trouble again for that.

On the way back he chalked up another "misdemeanor" by missing the train connection in Kiev, thanks to trying to see something of that city. When he arrived in Leningrad, he found the other dancers already deciding how his roles were likely to be shared among them, in the expectation of his dismissal.

He survived another two years in spite of that. There were more signs of official disfavor. Whenever foreign theater companies came to Russia (an American production of *My Fair Lady*, for instance, or the National Ballet of Cuba), Nureyev went to see them and tried to meet the performers. Perhaps because of this, when the American Ballet Theatre undertook a Russian tour in 1960, Nureyev was sent to travel around East Germany for a month with a circus troupe, dancing in poor conditions and going everywhere in a bus that broke down and stranded them for eight hours one night. Tired, cold and cramped, he was afraid of injuring himself again. Later the same year there was a trip with the same circus to the frozen north, traveling by train (a whole day and night in icy conditions) when he had been promised a plane. That infuriated him so much that he returned after one night. For this act of insubordination he was told that he would never again be permitted to dance before a senior government minister (which caused him no dismay) or to cross a foreign frontier.

The threat of being cut off from the outside world was disturbing. Already he had managed to make himself more open than his colleagues to outside influences. Having to miss seeing the Ballet Theatre performances because of his German tour, he left an 8mm film with a friend to record the dancing of their Danish star, Erik Bruhn, about whom he had already heard. When he saw it, he said, "It was a sensation for me. He is the only dancer who could impress me out of my wits. When I got back to Moscow, he had been dancing there, and one of the young dancers said he was too cool. Cool, yes—so cool that it burns."

During his time with the Kirov Nureyev gradually acquired more roles, amounting by the end of the three years to an impressive total. Among them were some of the big leading parts he has danced often in the West. In his second year with the company he took the male leads in *Don Quixote* and *Giselle.* The following year, he added the princes in *Swan Lake* and *The Sleeping Beauty;* he had already started to dance the Bluebird in the latter ballet and continued to alternate the two roles.

In addition, he played several roles he has never repeated outside Russia. One such was the hero Armen in Anisimova's *Gayane,* a ballet about love and adventure on a collective farm. He also prepared the leading part of Ferhad during the rehearsals of Yuri Grigorovich's *Legend of Love* but never had the chance to dance it in public. The ballet was a mixture of fairy story and political moralizing, based on a play by a Turkish author. But, as Nureyev remembers the circumstances, at that time "I was cast to dance often with Alla Shelest, another of the older ballerinas. She was another very good dancer, and hardworking, and I enjoyed working with her. But I think it was because of this that I did not dance *Legend of Love*. At one time it was thought I would perform the premiere, and I got as far as dancing one dress rehearsal, but Shelest had been Grigorovich's first wife, they were going through their divorce, and I don't know whether someone planned to put us together a lot with this in mind, but somehow if it was a plot it worked, and I was never cast to dance the ballet."

There were, however, several smaller roles that came his way: as one of the men in the pas de quatre in *Raymonda*; in a revival of *The Red Poppy* (dancing another pas de quatre with Soloviev, Sokolov and Seliutsky), and as Andrei, vying in heroic feats with his brother Ostap in the Cossack camp scene from *Taras Bulba*. (In the complete ballet, Andrei turns traitor for love of the Polish commander's daughter, but Nureyev only ever danced the one showpiece scene.) In concert performances he danced the duet from *Chopiniana* and a couple of small pieces specially created for him and Alla Sizova by Leonid Yakobson. In addition, he danced those celebrated Russian showoff numbers *Moszkovsky Waltz* and the pas de deux from *The Flames of Paris*, which, he says, did not suit him at all.

In all his big classic roles, incidentally, Nureyev danced with more than one of the Kirov ballerinas at different times, and he is proud of having partnered so many of them in those three years. In *Laurencia* he appeared with Shelest, as well as Dudinskaya; Shelest and Irina Kolpakova were his two Giselles. In *Swan Lake* he played opposite no fewer than four different ballerinas: Ninel Kurgapkina, Olga Moiseyeva, Alla Osipienko and Inna Zubkovskaya; all but the first of these appeared with him also in *La Bayadère,* and both Kurgapkina and Zubkovskaya played Kitri to his Basilio in *Don Quixote.* In *The Sleeping Beauty,* his Auroras were Kurgapkina and Xenia Ter-Stepanova; with the latter he also danced *Nutcracker,* while continuing to partner Sizova sometimes in that and in several smaller roles. When Russian dancers come to the West, we see them dancing mostly in set partnerships, so it is surprising that Nureyev was already so accustomed to adapting himself to different partners even before he left Russia. Most of these ballerinas, incidentally, were at Le Bourget on the fateful morning when he left the company, and during the tense period of waiting, wondering what best to do, they were in tears, even one or two with whom he had not been on specially close terms.

With so many roles to prepare and perform, so many partners to rehearse with, Nureyev must have been kept busy. The previous generation of Russian dancers had astonished their Western colleagues, when they first came to London and Paris, with tales of the long rehearsal periods they had in which to prepare new roles, but it is obvious that from the start Nureyev must have worked as quickly on his parts as any Western dancer. Nowadays the speed with which he can learn a completely new role is enviable; the complex and intricate rhythms of *Agon,* for instance, took him only four days to master, days during which he was also occupied in dancing other roles.

In those early years with the Kirov, as now, he was not just blindly copying what others had done but was bringing his own interpretation to the parts. One example is provided by the extra solo he introduced into *Giselle* after obtaining the approval of Grigorovich, who was in charge of the Kirov production at that time. Another instance came when he danced the role of Solor in the old ballet *La Bayadère*. This tale of love, jealousy and intrigue, in an Indian setting, was originally in five acts but the last (with its spectacular destruction of the temple) no longer survives, and only one scene, the Kingdom of Shades, has been given outside Russia.

A photograph I had, showing Chabukiani wearing a very elaborate old-fashioned costume for this role, prompted Nureyev to remark, "I wore that—the first time I danced the ballet." That led me to question him about the changes that had been made in the work at various times, by him and others. He explained, "Originally, you know, there was no solo in Act Four, the Kingdom of Shades, which is nowadays the last, although there should be another act after it, in accordance with the usual structure of these old ballets. This scene is supposed to be Solor's dream, so when people say he should not dance himself, they are right. But a solo had for quite a time been put into the finale, and I included the double assemblés in it. When this scene was given on its own in Paris, Sergeyev suggested I should put in another solo, but he did not say which, and on the first night I danced my *Corsair* solo and had a big success. But then I took Solor's solo from an earlier act of the ballet. I think the choreography of this must be by Chabukiani, who revised the ballet in the 1930s. He did not have a big jump, although he gave the illusion of this by his ballon, and he danced that solo much faster than I do. When I first came to dance the ballet, I asked if I could slow it down to show off my elevation, but I found the old costume restricting for this. So I did a sketch of something much simpler and showed it to Simon Virsaladze, who was the chief designer of the Kirov at that time. He approved it and made some suggestions about color, and then it was made up for me to wear. Now I suppose everyone will say that already I had begun to destroy everything!"

Ironically, when Nureyev left the Kirov, it was his version that was followed by the dancer who took over the role for the London season, wearing more or less his costume too, and this was taken by all of us as the yardstick against which to judge his own later revival for the Royal Ballet. Thus, like Chabukiani in an earlier generation, with whom he was often compared, Nureyev at twenty-three was already putting his own stamp firmly on certain roles. The belief that ballets can and should be reinterpreted is something that Nureyev has always been prepared to defend. "I don't think the public wants to see one good dancer after another, all exactly alike. It is only when some individual quality is there that it becomes interesting."

Because of the threat he had received about no more foreign travel, Nureyev did not expect to be chosen for the casts to be taken on the Kirov Ballet's first visit to Paris and London in the summer of 1961. A possible hint of whose influence may have affected how he did in fact get to Paris came at an embassy party on the company's arrival, when Ekaterina Furtseva, the Soviet Minister of Culture, singled him out for special attention and said that she expected to see him dance a lot during the season.

About a month before the trip, Sergeyev had been instructed that neither he nor his wife, Dudinskaya, were to dance. This came as a shock because, although he was fifty-one and she nearly forty-nine, they still appeared regularly and were the company's official leading dancers. Six years earlier, in fact, there had been a controversy when three leading members of the company wrote to *Pravda* complaining that this couple gave no chances to younger dancers. Perhaps someone in high authority was influenced by echoes of this, or possibly it was remembered that apart from Ulanova, the old-style dancers had tended to enjoy less success than their younger colleagues when the Bolshoi Ballet was in London. That could explain why other senior dancers who had originally been announced for the Kirov tour were also left out. Whatever the reason, the decree was absolute and was not relaxed even when the London ballet critics signed a petition begging for the veterans to dance just one performance. A petition from the gallery audience about the cast for *The Sleeping Beauty* on the last night of the season, asking for Yuri Soloviev to dance Bluebird, was granted, so it was not a question of the management's refusing on principle to listen to requests, only of declining the particular one about Dudinskaya and Sergeyev. Incidentally, further evidence of some feeling within the company against the Sergeyevs came early the following year when the leading ballerinas sent another letter to a newspaper, *Izvestia* this time, again complaining that young talent was being stifled. On the other hand, Nureyev, although naturally glad to have so many opportunities himself, has told me more than once that he thought Sergeyev should have been allowed to dance in London.

Because of the ban on Sergeyev, Nureyev was picked to dance several roles in Paris. He alternated with other dancers and was not, for instance, shown on the season's opening night, when Vladilen Semenov partnered Kolpakova in *The Sleeping Beauty*. But Nureyev had been cast for the preceding *répétition générale,* which in Paris is traditionally attended by many of the most influential people. Later he took the male leads in two other full evening ballets, *Swan*

Lake and *Giselle.* On programs of shorter works, he was seen in the Kingdom of Shades from *La Bayadère,* an extract from *The Nutcracker* and the Cossack camp scene from *Taras Bulba.* The company as a whole was enthusiastically received, but Nureyev's personal success with the French audiences was enormous, and because of this, it was decided that he was to dance the first night of each of those works when the company appeared at Covent Garden. Those people in the company and its management who did not approve of Nureyev's nonconformity can hardly have been pleased.

Also, he continued in Paris to behave outside the theater in ways which were not approved. While the other dancers dutifully went everywhere together in a company bus, Nureyev went off alone to concerts, art galleries and other places which interested him. He associated freely with French people, including one or two dancers from the Opéra, and other foreigners, making a number of new friends. Some of these were thought especially undesirable, in particular Clara Saint, a Chilean girl who was engaged to Vincent Malraux, one of the sons of the French Minister of Culture. Nureyev was warned against seeing them but took little or no notice.

The season at the Paris Opéra was followed by a further series of performances at the Palais des Sports, a huge arena in the southern suburbs. After that, the company was to fly to London on Saturday, June 17, for its Covent Garden season. At the airport Sergeyev came up to Nureyev and casually told him that he would not be traveling with the rest of them; he was needed at home for a special performance at the Kremlin and was to catch the Aeroflot flight to Moscow instead. Nureyev's suspicion had already been aroused on the airport bus when everyone had been given his own

flight ticket, a departure from the company's normal practice. Then they were collected up again.

That apparently pointless procedure seemed to Nureyev
the prelude to some mischief, and when he heard that he
was not flying to London after all, he interpreted the showing of his ticket as an attempt to lull him into a false sense
of security. He did not believe Sergeyev's assurance that he
would rejoin the company in London in a few days; he was
sure he would never be allowed out of the USSR again and
sure, too, that he would be squeezed out of the Kirov Ballet.
The way he saw the prospect was "Back to Ufa! Already I
had been sent away twice when I should have done important performances in Leningrad. I would never have been
allowed to dance in Leningrad or Moscow again, I am sure;
perhaps in small theaters three thousand miles away, but I
would have been squeezed off the stage eventually."

The agitation of other members of the company suggested that they shared his assessment of the situation, although they responded in different ways. The ballerinas
were in tears, but only Oleg Sokolov among the men
showed sympathy. Friends told Nureyev not to do anything
rash, but he recognized two plainclothes Soviet policemen
who had been following him around Paris and felt that he
was already virtually under arrest. One policeman stood by
the customs gate, the other by the main door, thus cutting
off escape in either direction. It might be that, if he still had
any doubts in his mind about what to do, that fact helped
Nureyev to decide, because from childhood, when other
children jostled him at school, he has always hated to be
hemmed in and instinctively tries to get away.

Consequently, he kept out of sight behind a pillar. He had
asked another dancer to telephone his friend Clara and say
good-bye for him. She took the hint that something was

amiss and drove immediately to the airport. When he saw her approaching, he called out to her that he had decided what to do. Guessing his meaning, she fetched two French police inspectors, who, in accordance with protocol, took him to a small room where he was left alone. The room had two doors, one back to the departure lounge, one to the inspectors' office, and he had to wait for a while without pressure while deciding which door to take. Attempts by one of the Soviet police and by an embassy official to interrupt were quietly ignored.

Left alone, Nureyev thought of the friends he would be leaving behind if he did not return to Russia and of the theater where he had hoped to make his career, but he also thought of the little niggling attacks which had made life difficult for him there. He thought of the fact that in the West he would be alone, working in conditions which might not meet the standards he thought right. But he could not bear the thought of not dancing, and all his life he had wanted to make his own individual contribution to the art, to express the feelings that were in his nature. He went out through the door that led to the French inspectors.

Nureyev's luggage was already on the way to London with the company, never to be seen again by its owner, and he was in Paris with about 50 francs (roughly $10) in his pocket. Friends put him up, the French authorities gave him permission to stay, and less than one week later, on Friday, June 23, he danced his first performance with a Western company, partnering Nina Vyroubova in the production of *The Sleeping Beauty* by the International Ballet of the Marquis de Cuevas. That same night the Kirov Ballet danced the first *Sleeping Beauty* of its Covent Garden season, which might otherwise have provided Nureyev's London debut.

The quick transition from one company to another makes it all sound easy. It was not. Obtaining his papers took only a few days. The offer of a contract with the Cuevas company was no surprise because Nureyev had already become a big star for the Paris audience. He had also already met Raymundo de Larrain, the nephew of the recently deceased marquis. Larrain had designed their latest spectacular production and was now looking after the company for his aunt, the marquise.

But although outwardly all was going well, Nureyev was only at the start of his troubles arising from the transition. For one thing, he did not approve of Larrain's ornate decors for *The Sleeping Beauty* and had argued with him that the style of the production was all wrong. When he went onstage that first night, dressed in an elaborate fringed tunic, with white wig and diamanté tiara, he felt (as he remarked later) "like a Christmas tree."

Offstage, he was harassed all the time. Men in raincoats followed him about, including the two whom he had identified at the airport as Soviet plainclothes police. As protection, Larrain hired a couple of detectives, whose presence was no less irksome. Everything Nureyev did was news, so reporters pestered him for interviews, often at times when all he wanted was to get on with his work or to be left in peace. Letters and telegrams arrived from his mother, his father, his teacher Pushkin, who had been like a second father. The tone varied from one to another, sorrowful, angry or warning, but the message in each was the same: he was making a terrible mistake. At one performance, a demonstration was arranged while he was dancing; people shouted and whistled and even threw what looked like broken glass on the stage. However, that particular incident in fact strengthened his resolve to stay, by showing the inconsistency of those who acted unscrupulously from what were supposed to be high-minded motives. He did not even feel afraid, only a strange serenity, and afterward he felt happier.

The Cuevas company at that time was presenting a straight run of *The Sleeping Beauty* instead of the usual mixed repertory. Nureyev appeared alternately (just as he had done with the Kirov) as the Prince and in the virtuoso Bluebird duet. He enjoyed his work, especially with Rosella Hightower, an American dancer who had been one of the company's ballerinas since its early days, gifted with an exceptionally strong technique, intelligent and receptive, too. But he found neither the company nor its audience very serious about ballet, and that troubled him. He had signed a contract for six months and did not renew it.

Luckily, there was no lack of other opportunities. The first of them came while he was still on the Cuevas strength. The company was appearing, after its Paris season, on some small stages where Nureyev would have felt too cramped to dance well, so he begged leave of absence. He went first to Frankfurt to appear on a television program—an unhappy occasion because when he arrived to film *Le Spectre de la rose,* there was nobody to teach him the part. When the producer eventually arrived, he expressed surprise that Nureyev did not already know the role. "Everybody knows it!" he said, to which the only possible answer was, "I don't." In the end the French dancer Pierre Lacotte was able to show him some movements, and Nureyev had to improvise the rest from studying photographs of Nijinsky. To make matters worse, both *Spectre* and the extracts from *Giselle* which were included in the program had to be danced to phonograph records, so the tempi left a great deal to be desired. "Mickey Mouse music" was Nureyev's succinct description.

However, from Frankfurt he went to Copenhagen, probably with three motives. For one thing, Erik Bruhn (whose dancing he already admired so much from the short film he had) was giving some guest performances with the Royal Danish Ballet. Also, there was in Copenhagen a Russian teacher, Vera Volkova, who had studied in Leningrad and still taught on lines similar to those practiced there. Finally, in a comparatively small city where he had never appeared, Nureyev would be able to get away from the fuss that constantly surrounded him in Paris, which had brought him to a state described by one person who first met him then as being "like a frightened animal."

In Copenhagen he found peace, mixed with curiosity and some alarm. Erik Bruhn told me how, when he came to take classes with Volkova at the Royal Theater, Nureyev used one of the dressing rooms to change, "and nobody except me spoke to him because he was very different from all us Danish boys, rather strange, and perhaps they were frightened of him."

Bruhn, ten years older than Nureyev, had left his native Copenhagen early in his career to become an international star, so he had already faced the problems of adaptation and self-sufficiency which Nureyev was just entering. Consequently, he was able to help the newcomer in many practical ways. What brought them together in a lasting friendship, however, was the recognition of each other's qualities. Although many people over the years have called Nureyev the greatest living male dancer, he himself always applied that description to Bruhn. In many respects the two men could hardly have been less alike. Nureyev at that time danced with a frenzied intensity, Bruhn with a calm perfection. That, at least, was the way it looked on the surface, but both were inspired by the same search for an unattainable ideal. Bruhn was the one male dancer in the West whose talents Nureyev could admire and emulate without reservation, the one in whom he saw qualities he was after. How much he has gained as an artist from working with Bruhn can be seen in the transformation of his style over the years, which I shall try to describe later. Bruhn for his part told me how much inspiration he gained from Nureyev's burning drive.

It is not often that one finds two such exceptional talents working together, and the results were incalculable. It was while working in Copenhagen, too, that Nureyev first heard from Margot Fonteyn, another great dancer with whom he was to be so rewardingly associated over the years. Fonteyn wanted him for a matinee at Drury Lane in aid of the Royal Academy of Dancing. The first contact was made through Volkova, whom Nureyev had grown to trust after some early hesitations which arose because the style of the Leningrad school had changed over the years since she studied there and consequently he found some of her ways surprising. It helped a good deal in their relationship when Nureyev discovered that Volkova had actually danced, many years before, with his admired teacher Pushkin.

Volkova had been one of Fonteyn's earliest teachers, had known her, in fact, since she was a child in Shanghai. One day, Volkova told me, Fonteyn unexpectedly telephoned her. "She asked, 'Vera, do you known where this Russian boy is?' I replied yes, he is right here in Copenhagen, and she asked me to invite him to dance at her gala. When I spoke to him, I had to explain that there would be no fee, just his expenses. He would go, he said, if he could dance with Margot, and suggested *Spectre de la rose*. When I informed Margot of this, she said, 'But I'm already dancing

Spectre with John Gilpin. Besides, I've never seen this boy, and I am not sure we should suit each other.' In the end, I said she had better speak to him on the phone herself, which she did, and invited him to come to London for a few days to arrange everything."

That visit was made incognito, and when Fonteyn took Nureyev to attend class at the Royal Ballet School, she pretended that he was a young student and gave him an assumed name, taken from one of the Polish dancers who were due to appear at the gala, although in the end they did not arrive. Thus it was as a Mr. Jasman, which somehow got changed to Jasmine (Jas for short) that Nureyev first entered the Royal Ballet's doors. He was sent, however, to the male principals' dressing room to change, where David Blair found him and asked, "You're that Russian, aren't you?" Nureyev stuck firmly to his alias and was therefore directed to a less exalted changing room, although it is difficult to believe that anybody was fooled for long once he got into the classroom.

Already on that first visit Nureyev found time to explore London on his own and to go at least twice to the ballet. He saw Ballet Rambert dance *Giselle,* and when Marie Rambert remarked that the standard of dancing in her small company must be very different from what he was used to, he delighted her by picking out the positive qualities he found in the performance. He admired Lucette Aldous in the title role ("She has nice legs; *edible* legs") and John Chesworth's acting as Hilarion. He went to Covent Garden, too, where Fonteyn was dancing the same ballet. She asked two old friends, the former dancer Maude Lloyd and her art-critic husband, Nigel Gosling (who jointly write about ballet under the pseudonym Alexander Bland), to collect Nureyev from her home and escort him to the theater. On arrival, they were astonished to find a sleepy tousle-haired young man in a dark sports shirt and tight trousers. They were wondering how they would manage to slip unobtrusively into the Royal Opera House with him, but after a smiling apology that he had been asleep, he transformed himself within five minutes into a smooth, handsome figure in a neat dark suit. The quick changes sometimes necessary onstage are something he carries into private life.

Already in a short space of time he had met two of the people, Bruhn and Fonteyn, who were to have most influence on his career, and a third soon came on the scene: Frederick Ashton, who agreed to create a new solo for Nureyev's London debut. The dancer himself chose the music, from the *Poème tragique* by one of his favorite composers, Alexander Scriabin, and was amused when people tried to read tragic implications into it. In fact, the solo was heroic in mood. He wore streaky gray tights, with a red and white ribbon bound around one shoulder, across his bare chest and around his waist. The dance was quite short: Nureyev rushed forward to the front of the stage, then hurtled into a short, fast sequence of fiendishly difficult steps. What left the most abiding impression, however, was not his virtuosity, but his temperament and dramatic quality. There were plenty of people to point out that if Nureyev jumped high, he sometimes landed heavily, and that his tours en l'air were not always strictly vertical, but there was no missing the deep fires that burned in his eyes or the strangely relaxed intensity which hinted at more exciting things to come when we saw him in a major role.

Similarly with the "Black Swan" pas de deux from *Swan Lake* which he danced with Hightower later in the program: it was an uneven but exciting performance. Incidentally, the program book had stated that they would perform the pas de deux from *Don Quixote,* and no announcement of the alteration was made. One reviewer the next morning had actually failed to notice the difference, so it is possible that quite a few people have the wrong idea of what they first saw him dance. Audience response was delirious, so much so that Nureyev had to repeat his solo in the pas de deux (something he will very rarely do), and the acclaim of Paris was repeated in London.

One consequence of this gala was that Nureyev was invited back to London to dance three performances of *Giselle* with the Royal Ballet, and this time he was to partner Fonteyn. But first he had to work out the balance of his contract with the Cuevas Ballet, and there was also an unusual venture which he and three friends had decided to undertake on their own initiative. Bruhn, Hightower and Sonia Arova were the others. Born in Bulgaria but brought up in France, Arova had made her early career with British ballet companies before dancing as ballerina with many others in Europe and America. The four of them decided to prepare a complete concert program for themselves. Such gala concerts are not uncommon in France, but this one differed from others in the small number involved and because, instead of dancing mostly extracts from existing works, they created the bulk of the program specially for the occasion. Bruhn described to me how they went about it: "Rosella had just opened her studio in Cannes, and it had not had time to get a lot of pupils, so we were able to work uninterrupted from about one thirty in the afternoon until eleven thirty at night, taking class and then choreographing and rehearsing. We had three big pieces on the program in which all four of us appeared and two pas de deux. I don't think we could possibly have managed more than the four performances we gave, two in Cannes and two in Paris, because it was so strenuous, but it was a marvelous experience to work in that way, doing what we wanted."

Bruhn created two ensemble pieces for the program. In the opening *Toccata and Fugue,* plotless dances to music by Bach, there was a section where, he told me, "Rudik and I danced identical steps but starting from opposite sides. Sometimes we had our backs to each other while we were dancing, but we did it all exactly alike in spite of having very different physique and schooling. This can be done—that's why I find it unforgivable when people cannot keep in time." Bruhn's other contribution closed the program: a lighthearted *Fantaisie* about four young people meeting in a park and indulging in flirtation, jealousy or romantic reverie. Oddly enough, although the music was by three Spanish composers, the solos comprised two mazurkas for the women, a schottische for Nureyev and a passacaglia for Bruhn.

Nureyev's contributions to the production were a pas de quatre to music from *Raymonda* and the two pas de deux, from *The Nutcracker* and from *Don Quixote,* which he danced with Hightower. It is interesting that all these were extracts from works which he later staged in their entirety.

The idea that he would eventually produce ballets had been in his mind right from the beginning of his career. While still at school, he told me, "I wrote down all of *Les Sylphides.* I don't know why; I think maybe I had the idea that one day I would go back to Ufa and mount all these ballets. Then I found just the last page of my notes hanging in the loo: you can imagine what the rest had been used for. That cured me. It was the last time I tried to record things in that way. One remembers them."

His first real attempt at production was made on tour in Israel with the Cuevas company. "It was *Nutcracker* pas de deux, and I worked it all out on paper, wrote everything down and made sure of all the details. We got hold of a tiny little theater in Haifa, and Rosella Hightower lent herself for experiment. I think it was fantastic that she was willing to make herself available in that way and try out all sorts of things." The extent to which Nureyev had worked on the choreography was not generally realized at the time. When Hightower and he danced *The Nutcracker* duet on BBC television, for instance, no special credit was given for the choreography, and there are so many different versions extant that there was no reason for anyone to guess this one was his own.

The concert program had its first performance in Cannes on January 6, 1962. The previous night Hightower and Nureyev had been to Marseilles, a hundred miles along the coast, to dance with the local company in a production of *La Fille mal gardée* by their director, Joseph Lazzini. At that time Nureyev danced often with small, comparatively unknown companies. Not that he was hard up for work; it was already being suggested, for instance, that he should star in a film about Nijinsky, an idea mooted hopefully but vainly by many producers and directors over the years. But what always mattered most to Nureyev was fresh and valuable experience. Even much later, when his schedules became both crowded and complex, he would go to enormous trouble to dance an interesting new role.

The gala concert had a second performance in Cannes, then two in Paris the following week at the Théâtre des Champs-Élysées. Not all the reviews were enthusiastic (one asserted that the evening consisted of dancing, hysterical applause and intervals in more or less equal parts), but the success of the venture was not for a moment in doubt. There were plenty of offers to tour the program, which could undoubtedly have been extremely profitable. If they had been accepted, the enterprise might easily have grown willy-nilly into a full-scale company, and some of Nureyev's friends think that his talents would have found their fullest expression in directing a company. But there would have been risks of artistic stagnation, and Nureyev would have missed the formative experience of his partnership with Fonteyn. In any event, the four dancers decided not to continue because, as Bruhn explained it, "there would not have been the same freedom to work as we wanted." He added, incidentally, that "we spent two months preparing the concert, and the house was sold out each night, but by the time we had paid all the costs for music and costumes and so on we had about one hundred and fifty dollars each out of the takings." It is just as well that they enjoyed their work.

On the day of the second Paris performance Bruhn hurt his foot. He managed to dance in the three ensemble works, although he had to omit his solos from the Glazunov and Spanish pieces. But it was impossible for him to attempt the pas de deux from *Flower Festival at Genzano,* which he was due to dance with Arova in his own adaptation of August Bournonville's original nineteenth-century choreography. Nureyev knew this piece only from having seen Bruhn preparing and dancing it, but he rapidly rehearsed it and went on in his friend's place as well as danced all his own roles.

That incident led directly to Nureyev's American debut, because Bruhn was under contract to dance the duet the following week with Maria Tallchief on television in New York. Again Nureyev took his place, this time with more rehearsal. The style and technique of this classical showpiece in the old Franco-Danish style were entirely different from anything he was used to in the USSR. Modern Soviet choreography and their productions of the classics alike tend to rely on a few big, powerful steps with rests in between. Bournonville used many quick, small steps. At first, Nureyev found these difficult, but he managed them and over the years deliberately set out to master this aspect of technique, as he had already done others.

Nureyev's Covent Garden debut came on February 21, 1962. The bombardment of publicity surrounding the occasion was immense. When Lord Snowdon was allowed to take photographs for the *Sunday Times* of Fonteyn and Nureyev rehearsing at the Royal Ballet's studios, other photographers protested at the special treatment. Frederick Ashton, who had produced *Giselle* for the Royal Ballet, was interviewed and said, "Changes and adaptations have been made. . . . It would have been absurd and lacking in imagination and tact to have attempted to squeeze Nureyev into a preconceived mold." Those changes were soon to be the subject of fierce controversy.

It is difficult to tell how much a performer is helped, and how much hindered, by the sort of publicity Nureyev had then. When people have been told in advance that they are going to see something extraordinary, some will convince themselves it was so even if the reports were exaggerated. Others will sit back, determined to prove their own balanced judgment by refusing to succumb.

Nureyev's interpretation of Albrecht swept up a storm of excitement. The general line of his approach was not new; he followed other recent Russian readings of the role by showing a thoughtless young aristocrat in Act 1, instead of the dashing romantic hero then usual in Western productions, and by stressing the anguish of remorse in Act 2. This conception of the character is easily justifiable on theoretical grounds as soon as one thinks about the historical and social background of the plot rather than just accept it as a medieval and supernatural love story. Nureyev's special contribution lay in making his actions and moods seem like a natural response to the dramatic situation and to the music. The detailed naturalism of his acting in the first act came as a revelation, and so did the way he soared through the solos in the second act. His cabrioles, especially, were not only far higher and traveled farther than any British dancer had managed, but he gave an illusion of pausing in the air at their highest point. His slight build and boyish appearance added to the effect of his performance; even more striking were the wild grace of his dancing and his complete absorption in every moment of the action.

Also, even at that first performance together, Nureyev's presence had a transforming effect on Fonteyn. Giselle had not been one of her greatest roles, partly because she danced it less often than the other classic heroines, but Nureyev's alertness to every nuance and the conviction of his acting stirred her to a new liveliness in the part. At the end of the evening they took twenty-three curtain calls. At one of them Fonteyn was presented with a big bunch of roses. Choosing one, she kissed it and handed it to her new partner—a customary gesture which was transformed into something personal and touching when he dropped instantly to his knees and kissed her hand.

A great partnership had been born, but there were rumblings of discontent among the acclamation. It would have been silly for anyone to object to the new ending which Nureyev imposed on the ballet, with Albrecht kneeling alone on the stage, grieving for his lost love. This was patently better than the Royal Ballet's previous version, and variants were soon adopted by all the casts. But Nureyev also, following what he had learned in the Soviet Union, adopted different choreography for several entries in Act 2 and even introduced his own new solo for Albrecht at a moment when he is generally offstage. Actually, this solo—bounding up and down in a series of entrechats while the Wilis dance around him—makes dramatic sense and has since been widely copied. It helps show the hero trapped by these ghosts of dead girls, and it also underlines the idea that they are trying to dance him to death from exhaustion. At the time, however, many spectators, especially critics and other dancers, were shocked at the idea of anyone's arbitrarily changing the traditional choreography of this and other standard works. It was regarded as a precious heritage and the foundation of a classical tradition in Britain. The national ballet at that time was too young for people to feel happy about taking risks with what had been achieved.

The person who deserves special credit for supporting Nureyev at that time was, by a stroke of irony, the one who had done more than anyone else to build up the traditions which the newcomer was accused of endangering. It was Ninette de Valois, founder and director of the Royal Ballet, who insisted on inviting him to work with the company, although there were many among her colleagues who thought it too risky. Her justification has been the vitalizing effect his example had on British male dancing, as well as his contributions to the repertory and the intrinsic value of his performances.

After those first three performances with the Royal Ballet, Nureyev was quickly invited back, and the company has been the one to which he returned most frequently over the years, providing the nearest he had to a home base. But before he danced again in London, he made his American stage debut on March 10, not in one of the major New York theaters but at the Brooklyn Academy of Music. The occasion was the only New York appearance that season of Ruth Page's Chicago Opera Ballet. Arova was dancing with the company as guest star, and Nureyev partnered her in the *Don Quixote* pas de deux. The sold-out house, the wild applause and the general enthusiasm of the reviews, coupled with some recognition of the fact that he was still young and not yet fully formed as a dancer, repeated the pattern established in London.

In a conversation after the performance with Anatole Chujoy, editor of the American newspaper *Dance News*, Nureyev more than hinted a wish to work regularly in New York. He expressed his admiration for the ballets of George Balanchine, artistic director of New York City Ballet, saying, "Mr. Balanchine's ballets are a new field for me, very different from the field where I work now, and I should like to know it better. It would be perfect for me if Mr. Balanchine would accept my working with the Royal Ballet part of the year and with the New York City Ballet part of the year." If the suggestion had been taken up, his later career might have been very different, but Balanchine made no response to that or later approaches.

Nureyev's next series of performances in London began on May 3, at the annual gala in aid of the Royal Ballet Benevolent Fund. The Royal Ballet had never had so many guest stars at once. Arova, Bruhn, Nureyev and the French ballerina Yvette Chauviré all were engaged that summer. Again Nureyev caused controversy with a new solo he introduced into *Swan Lake.* Set to the Andante sostenuto written for (but not used in) the pas de trois, this was a dreamy, melancholy number intended to show the hero's mood. It was entirely new. In Leningrad, he later told me, he had tried to convey the same mood simply by walking about the stage with a mandolin at that point in the action. The experiment was not entirely successful, but in subsequent productions, when Nureyev had polished his choreography and it was fitted more carefully into the general action, it worked much better.

It was in a performance of *Swan Lake* (not with Nureyev) that one of the company's ballerinas, Nadia Nerina, made the most amusing of the many comments on the changes he was introducing into the classics. During the pas de deux in Act 3 she suddenly grinned and performed thirty-two entrechats (which, at least in series, are generally a man's step) instead of the customary thirty-two fouettés.

In fact, Nureyev's other two changes that season were not controversial. One was the introduction of a different solo for Prince Florimund in *The Sleeping Beauty*. This was the version which had for many years been danced by the Kirov Ballet, and it was adopted by the Royal Ballet for general use. Nureyev was not even the first to dance it for them, having taught it to other men in the company before his own London debut in the role. In *Les Sylphides,* which he danced for the first time at the gala, he naturally introduced the solo he had learned, but never publicly performed, in Leningrad, to the mazurka Op. 67 No. 3 instead of Op. 33 No. 3 as in most Western productions. But that was known to be an alternative instigated by the choreographer, Mikhail Fokine, so nobody could complain. Actually, the Russian version seems to me so much stronger, although more difficult, that I am surprised it has not been adopted by other dancers, too.

During that season, Nureyev had several different partners: Fonteyn for *Giselle,* Arova for *Swan Lake* and the *Don Quixote* pas de deux, and Chauviré in *Les Sylphides* and *The Sleeping Beauty.* The last named was unfortunately past the peak of her career and no longer ideally suited to these roles. One or two minor mishaps occurred, and when Chauviré had to withdraw from one of her scheduled performances of *The Sleeping Beauty*, there were plenty of people ready to suggest that they did not get on well together and that Nureyev had been either clumsy or deliberately careless. It was easy to deduce the complete lack of justification for those stories from the fact that she invited him to dance with her again at a gala in Stuttgart later that summer, for which he learned one of her special showpieces, the *Grand Pas classique* which had been created for her by Victor Gsovsky.

In fact, the alleged lack of rapport between them was so far from the truth that Nureyev was astonished, even incredulous, when he read about it in the first draft of this book. However unjustified, there were by now a lot of mutterings and complaints about his supposed high-handedness and bad behavior. Some of them took the form of suggestions that although Nureyev might perform certain technical tricks very well, British dancers had more artistry and discipline. Typical was a letter published in the weekly theatrical paper *The Stage*, which declared tartly that "it takes more than good elevation and bad stage manners to make a genius."

Part of the trouble was undoubtedly caused by the fact that Michael Somes, who for some years had been Fonteyn's usual partner, had recently retired and it had appeared that David Blair, a talented and highly popular younger dancer, would take his place. Blair did, in fact, dance with Fonteyn on various occasions, and although they proved rather less than ideally matched, Blair's many admirers naturally resented the idea of their favorite being squeezed out, as they thought, by the newcomer.

There were other factors. It is true that Nureyev, like most people, is likely to lose his temper sometimes, and by working as hard as he does and caring so much about his work, he increases the stress on himself. Consequently, he can flare up alarmingly. I have seen him at a rehearsal, when a pianist repeatedly took no notice of requests for a different tempo, fly into a rage and use some extremely vehement expressions. But before that point was reached, he had already tried in vain to get some response from the unfortunate pianist both by quiet explanation and by humor ("You speak English?" he asked in a deliberately heavy accent). And having given vent to his feelings, a few moments later he was as calm as ever. As Fonteyn said when asked, in the film *I Am a Dancer*, about his personality: "It's complex and very simple and always interesting. Very often he's very amusing, and one was never going to be bored with him. He has a lot of changes of mood. Sometimes they're bad, but they're not really serious. He does not mean them—he means them at the time, but in five minutes it's gone."

In addition, Nureyev's complete, all-absorbing concentration on trying to get his own performances right could easily look, to people who did not know him, like conceit or rudeness. It must be remembered, too, that when he first arrived in the West, he was very young. Abruptly, he found himself precipitated from a society where life was full of constraints to another where attitudes were very different. For the first time in his life, he had plenty of money in his pocket, he was surrounded by people who had backgrounds he did not know, and he was idolized on all sides. It would have been surprising if he had not sometimes been a little wild in consequence. But this has often been exaggerated and needs to be kept in proportion. Nowadays people who knew him in his earliest Western days often remark how much he has changed. To put that change into perspective, it is worth mentioning that, as early as the spring of 1963, Clive Barnes described Nureyev, in an article for the magazine *Town* about his influence on British ballet, as "a reformed character."

Also, his life was certainly not interfering with his work. After that Covent Garden season in the summer of 1962, he and Fonteyn had danced *Swan Lake* at the Nervi Festival in Italy with the Royal Ballet's smaller touring company. The beginning of the new theatrical season found him again in the United States. For television, he taught the woman's role in *The Corsair* pas de deux to Lupe Serrano, one of the ballerinas of the American Ballet Theatre, and danced it with her on the *Bell Telephone Hour*. While in New York for this, he startled many people by attending performances of the Bolshoi Ballet, which was giving a season there. That was somehow thought daring, but I am sure it would never have occurred to him not to go; he had no quarrel with Russian ballet.

Performances with the Chicago Lyric Opera and the Chicago Opera Ballet occupied much of October. The ballet company has never achieved an international reputation, but under Ruth Page's shrewd and knowledgeable direction, it annually undertook extensive tours of the United States, headed by guest stars. Nureyev, however, appeared only in Chicago, making his debut as the chief warrior in the Polovtsian dances in a production of the opera *Prince Igor* with Boris Christoff singing Khan Khonchak. The choreography for the dances was based on Fokine's famous version but with some added solo passages of virtuoso feats for Nureyev. He also danced Danilo in Page's balletic version of *The Merry Widow*, with Arova in the title part.

For a gala before leaving Chicago, he again mounted *The*

Corsair pas de deux, this time with Arova; then, on returning to London, he taught the role to Fonteyn. First given at
Covent Garden on November 3, it was a small but brilliantly successful beginning to his contributions to the Royal
Ballet's repertory, although not recorded as such in the program credits. These described the choreography simply as
"after Petipa," but he might well have had difficulty in rec-
ognizing it. The original ballet of *The Corsair*, with music
by Adolphe Adam (best known as the composer of *Giselle*),
was created in France by Joseph Mazilier, with an adventur-
ous story based on Byron's celebrated poem of the same title. Petipa revived it in Russia with many amendments and
additions, among them the showpiece which is all we usually see today. Even that began life, Nureyev tells me, as a
pas de trois, and among other adaptations since Petipa's
time the element of bravura display has been greatly in-
creased, notably by Chabukiani in the 1930s, who must
have been fond of his choreography for the man's solo, since
he incorporated it also (to different music) into another of
his ballets, *Gorda.*

In its present form, it is full of big jumps for the man, and
in this more than any other role Nureyev was able to display the soaring quality of his technique. In the solo the
lithe springiness with which he leaped to revolve in the air,
the smoothness of his pirouettes and the crispness of his
final circuit of the stage all contributed to a sense of ex-
hilaration. Then his long, high grands jetés in the finale always caused a gasp by the way he appeared to hover in the
air at their peak. Happily, he cajoled a bravura performance
from Fonteyn, too, in a solo carefully adjusted to fit her special qualities, so that although the piece was somewhat
different from her usual run of roles, she shared fully in the
triumph.

Nureyev's performances that winter were interrupted,

however, by two unfortunate incidents. First, he hurt his foot and had to cancel all appearances for a while (although he kept a commitment to film *Les Sylphides,* heavily bandaged). Covent Garden had just announced that he would be dancing with the Royal Ballet over the Christmas period, his roles to include the intended premiere of Ashton's *Marguerite and Armand* on December 13. An announcement was made about revised programs, attributing these entirely to Nureyev's injury. It so happened that news had just reached London of an announcement by the American Ballet Theatre that he would be appearing with the company in Chicago during the Christmas week. Some journalists on the *Daily Express* asked Covent Garden what would have happened about the clash of engagements if Nureyev had not hurt his foot. The press office there first admitted that Nureyev's Chicago dates had been known for some time, then said they had been instructed not to comment. The impression was given that, to save their own faces, some people at the Opera House were prepared for it to appear that Nureyev had been behaving irresponsibly, and the affair undoubtedly did unfairly exacerbate his reputation for wildness. His only comment was that he could not have broken any contract in London because he had no contract to break.

He had been due also to dance at Fonteyn's annual gala matinee for the Royal Academy of Dancing but was unable to do so and recommended Viktor Rona, a dancer from the Hungarian Ballet, to take his place partnering her in the pas de deux from *Gayane* which he had staged. To recuperate from his injury, he flew to Australia, then went on to Chicago, where, in addition to *The Corsair* with Serrano, he danced two new roles. One was Colin in another version of *La Fille mal gardée,* staged by Bronislava Nijinska; the other was his first in one of Balanchine's ballets: *Theme and Variations*, a plotless work in very strict classical style to music by Tchaikovsky, constructed to show off two star dancers with a supporting ensemble.

Toward the end of the year Nureyev's autobiography was published—rather early, as he was only twenty-four. He was not at all keen to write it but was persuaded by the argument that it would be good for his career. Already, even before leaving the Soviet Union, he had taught himself a smattering of English and French, but the book was composed by a series of interviews, not directly written by him. Reading it with hindsight, one can regret several occasions where the interviewer might have followed up remarks which were clearly of interest to Nureyev, but the brief was clearly to make as much as possible of the more sensational aspects of his "leap to freedom." All the same, it is remarkable how much of Nureyev himself emerges in the text, his clear-sighted attitude toward his career, his interest in whatever is happening around him, his generosity toward others.

Others were not always so generous toward him. About that time, at the beginning of 1963, he was due to dance some performances at the Paris Opera, but the Russian authorities put pressure on the French, threatening the end of other cultural exchanges, and his appearances there were canceled. The previous year a proposal for Maya Plisetskaya from the Bolshoi Ballet to dance at Covent Garden had come to nothing, but whether that was for a similar reason was never stated. However, Ruth Page told me that it was fear of reprisals against the cultural exchange program that kept Nureyev for some time from being invited to appear with major companies in New York.

Once back at Covent Garden, Nureyev danced a number

of new roles. Three of them he played only during that season, but another has become one of the parts with which he is most closely associated. First came Etiocles, one of the warring brothers in John Cranko's *Antigone*. Presumably that part was thought the more suitable for him because it needed a dancer with powerful physique and elevation (it had been created for the Rhodesian dancer Gary Burne), but it was too straightforward dramatically to offer much of interest for Nureyev to develop. The other brother, Polynices (created for Blair), who tries to stir up the people of Thebes to support him against Creon's plots, might possibly have provided more of a challenge. Next, he took the leading male part in Kenneth MacMillan's plotless ballet *Diversions*, to music by Arthur Bliss: its fast, fluent style was probably a useful exercise for him, being so different from anything he had done before, although it not surprisingly suited him less ideally than Donald MacLeary, for whose physique and abilities it was built.

Then in March came the postponed premiere of *Marguerite and Armand*. Ashton made this specifically for Fonteyn and Nureyev. Its creation was put off until they both were available, and nobody else has ever been allowed to dance the title parts. More than any other ballet, this for many people epitomizes the partnership of Fonteyn and Nureyev. They have toured it with the Royal Ballet, it has been mounted, with them, in several European cities, and it is included complete, with only slight adaptations, in the film *I Am a Dancer*. In the film, the pair of them and Ashton discussed how it came to be created:

Ashton: I'm a very romantic character, so naturally I'm drawn to romantic heroines and Marguerite Gautier is someone who has always fascinated me, and I read a great

66

deal about her. Then quite by accident I heard this sonata of Liszt's one day on the wireless [radio], and I sat there, and I saw the whole thing could be contained in this music. Margot seemed to me the epitome of Marguerite Gautier, and Rudolf seemed to me the epitome of Armand.

Nureyev (laughs): Well, I guess Fred has got a very good eye for type casting.

Ashton: He's a passionate human being, and Armand was a passionate human being. I am often accused that it is just merely a vehicle for two star performers, and I say, "Well, what's wrong with that?" I mean, Sarah Bernhardt had many vehicles written for her, and they were very successful, and she also was a great *Dame aux Camélias*.

Fonteyn: I can't imagine that it could feel better to be acting or singing the role. It's marvelous to dance it and, of course, to dance it with Rudolf. I also couldn't imagine dancing it with anybody else. I think it has to be Rudolf as Armand.

Nureyev: It was a very, very important moment, I would say, the first ballet being choreographed for me.

Ashton: I didn't want it all to be a realistic thing. I wanted it to be more an *évocation poétique*.

An example of how quick and responsive Nureyev was to work with was given by Ashton in the course of a long article by Alexander Bland, published in the *Observer* immediately before the premiere. Ashton described how, contrary to his usual practice of starting at the beginning and working methodically through, he decided to start with the highlights, the scenes with the two principals together. On the first day he worked on their first meeting and was delighted that it went well. Then "the next day I did one of the scenes with the father. Michael [Somes] was standing there with Margot, very stern and stiff, and I saw the door open a crack and Rudi looking in very cautiously, in his scarf and everything. I could see him tiptoe round behind me as we went on working, and when we began to come to the end of the scene he started stripping off his coat and things and just at the right moment he flew out from behind me into Margot's arms; it was wonderful."

In a radio interview Nureyev was asked how he had developed his characterization and replied that he had taken Robert Taylor as his model. The interviewer jumped to the conclusion that he must have seen the film of *Camille* since arriving in the West, and with the demurest hint of irony Nureyev corrected him: "We did have cinemas in Russia, you know."

Later that month Nureyev was due to dance another Ashton ballet, *Symphonic Variations,* but on the day he was suffering from a poisoned hand and could not go on. Another performance was due two nights later. Nobody expected him to appear, but at five in the afternoon he arrived at Covent Garden dosed with antibiotics. In that state he gave his only performance in what is one of the most jealously guarded of the Royal Ballet's works. It had been a landmark in the company's development when created during their first Covent Garden season in 1946, showing how the big stage could be used for pure dancing with only a small cast of three couples and no elaborate scenery. The delicate, lyrical choreographic invention, too, was taken as the hallmark of the distinctively British style. Nureyev's single performance was illuminating. In this ballet, any trace of a "Russian accent" would have been out of place. Nureyev's arm movements were softer than we had seen before in this role, but he danced simply and naturally in an entirely

"English" way. Also, the ballet revealed more than anything else the innate musicality of his dancing, which
shows not in matching gesture to beat, but in catching the
tone and shape of a whole phrase of music. That kind of
musical response, unfortunately, probably did not suit the
choreographer's conception of the work, based on the more
tightly organized timing customary among British dancers,
and Nureyev was never cast for the role again.

That summer Nureyev undertook his first American tour
with the Royal Ballet. He was by then regarded as a "permanent guest" with the company, not listed as a full member
but appearing frequently. Tactfully, the company avoided
playing too heavily on his presence for the New York season. On opening night, for instance, Blair partnered Fonteyn in *The Sleeping Beauty*. That did not prevent John
Martin, the dean of American dance critics, from launching
a strong attack in the *Saturday Review*. He accused Nureyev of acting, unintentionally, as a "disintegrating force"
and said of his partnership with Fonteyn that "she has gone,
as it were, to the grand ball with a gigolo." By now, however, that was very much a minority view. Most people
could see that, as well as the excitement of his own performances, his presence stimulated the other male dancers to
a higher standard, either by example or through competition.

In Toronto, later in the tour, Nureyev was again in the
news when, after a post-performance party, he walked
along the middle of the road at 3 A.M. For that he was arrested but soon released without any charges being brought, a
constable commenting, "He's a very emotional fellow and
not familiar with our by-laws" which showed a more sensible attitude than is sometimes found in such circumstances.

The importance in retrospect of these two incidents, Martin's attack and the Toronto arrest, is that the summer of 1963 was probably the last time when any reasonable person could have doubts about the benefit of Nureyev's influence. Before another year was out, he had begun to show his capacity as a producer, as well as notably to widen his repertory and consolidate his grasp of Western ways. The matter of adapting to the different circumstances of Western ballet was a complex one. Simplifying the difference, one might say that it is primarily concerned with the emphasis put on the relative importance of choreography and dancing—the conception, structuring and arrangement of the steps on the one hand, the way they are performed on the other. Since choreography cannot exist without dancing and since dancing would not be ballet without choreography, these are not opposed functions but two aspects of one whole. The way Nureyev put it to me was: "In Russia our dancing was less concerned with line than in the West. We had elaborate productions, well thought out and true to period detail: this was the legacy of Petipa. But dancing there was very emotionally charged, depending on performance, not structure."

You can see the contrast most strikingly in comparing a typical modern Soviet ballet with one in a Western repertory. The Bolshoi *Spartacus* uses rather simply structured (although technically difficult), repetitive solos and duets for its principals, but the emotional temperature of the performance is so high that one hardly notices that. It would be as difficult for a British or American cast to dance *Spartacus* with any kind of conviction as it would for the Russians to fit their broader, more impassioned style into the intricate, precisely ordered and decidedly cool patterns of Balanchine's *Agon* or Ashton's *Symphonic Variations*. The different approach extends even to the standard classics: dancing the same solo in *Swan Lake,* a Western dancer would probably perform more steps, while the Russian concentrated on a few spectacularly big ones, with poses or promenades between them.

That disjunction of styles which had a common origin in the old Imperial Russian Ballet reflects their different development in the light of varying social, economic and artistic circumstances. The differences have become more acute, I think, since the last world war. When the young Bolshoi ballerina Violetta Prokhorova was allowed to leave Russia with her British husband, Harold Elvin, and joined what was then the Sadler's Wells Ballet on its move to Covent Garden in February, 1946, she proved exotic in manner, as well as looks, but she appeared to fit without serious difficulty into the British company. However, the company itself was at that time changing fast. What is important is that an outsider may more easily be assimilated at the head of a company than lower down its ranks; differences of personality and other qualities are expected and welcomed among the principals but unacceptable in the corps de ballet.

For Nureyev, the adaptation had to be threefold: from the Russian way of life to that of the West, from a permanent position in a company to the risks and opportunities of a free lance, and from the Russian style of dancing to something different that would work in Western choreography. But complete acceptance of Western style would have been disastrous, since it was for his individual qualities that he was in demand. Luckily, his inquiring nature helped in the transition. He always wanted to ask the what, why and wherefore of every step. It was not that he lacked strong views of his own—in fact, those who worked with him found him quick to explain how he thought things could best be done—but he was willing to profit from their experience.

He said to me, "I had the baggage of knowledge, but how to operate with it I learned in England. When I came to the West, I found it necessary to hold onto everything that was good in what I had been taught, but to find ways of using it in different circumstances and assimilating new influences. I think I was capable of accepting things—not just taking Western style, but asking all the time 'Why?' When Makarova left the Kirov, I rehearsed with her to dance on television, and she said to me, 'You dance like them!' I told her 'No, I dance like me.' I think I have found my own balance, although it must be a perilous one. It is hard to find the right equilibrium within yourself. When I left Russia, they asked, 'What will you be without your teachers? Soon you will be nothing.' But I think teachers are for school. They gave me knowledge, and it was up to me to utilize it. And I think I gained a lot in the West. Here, if you have initiative, and the drive and tenacity to go right through, you're a winner."

One of the things he is most proud of is his partnership with Fonteyn, and rightly so, because two dancers, both already exceptional, were inspiring each other to fresh achievements. He learned much from her, and she from him. He commented to me, about their work together over the years, "It's not her, it's not me; it is the sameness of the goal. Some other people have added something also, especially Fred." When I asked him whether he would have liked to be able to dance again in Leningrad, he replied, "I would have liked to dance there with Margot, to show what we achieved."

That was one ambition he never achieved, but he and

Fonteyn did dance together in a remarkably large and widespread number of cities. Back in that summer of 1963, when a few people were still grumbling about how he was supposed to be spoiling her, they and a small supporting group spent the holiday period on tour with a concert program, including an extract from *La Sylphide*, which was new to both of them. After that, Fonteyn and he went to Paris, where they headed the Royal Ballet's touring company in *Swan Lake*.

Next came Nureyev's first attempt at the famous role of Petrushka, the tragic doll that mysteriously proves to have a soul. The result proved disappointing. Like other interpreters of the part with the Royal Ballet, he was taught it by Serge Grigoriev, former régisseur of the Diaghilev Ballet, who had been present at the creation of the work and subsequently for two decades was responsible for maintaining it in the Diaghilev repertory. Grigoriev was noted for his detailed memory of the old ballets but was less good at coaching. Consequently, although he learned a more authentic version of the Fokine choreography than is generally seen nowadays, Nureyev did not at that time get fully to grips with the character. His instinct and intelligence enabled him to make at least as much of it as anyone else during that period, in fact much more than most, but he could not bring that honest but dull production to life. This was a role he was to resume later with infinitely more success.

Then at the end of November, 1963, came his production of *La Bayadère* for the Royal Ballet. It would be fascinating to see the whole of this old ballet staged in London one day (the project is one which Nureyev advocates keenly), but the classical divertissement from the Kingdom of Shades scene is generally regarded in the Soviet Union as one of the perfect pieces remaining from Petipa's long reign in charge of the St. Petersburg ballet during the second half of the nineteenth century. Nureyev based his production on the version he had danced with the Kirov Ballet but made a few minor changes in mounting the work at Covent Garden. In particular, he replaced one passage for the corps de ballet with what he considered a more interesting dance (to a similar waltz rhythm, and therefore fitting the music without any difficulty) from another scene. But the revival was faithful, both in its outlines and in its detail, to what we had already seen the Kirov Ballet dance in London. Nureyev is one of the rare dancers with a gift of remembering not just the roles they have themselves danced, but everyone else's too. But the important thing about the revival was not merely the feat of memory involved in reproducing a ballet with two principals, three soloists and a corps de ballet of thirty-two dancers. He taught his cast not only the steps, but the style too.

That might sound too high a claim, since the company had included some of Petipa's ballets in its repertory right from its beginnings, but these had been transmuted into an essentially English translation of the original style: smaller-scaled, gentle and lyrical. For *La Bayadère,* Nureyev encouraged his soloists to a sharper, more diamond-bright attack, and in the long opening dance, with its procession of arabesques down a steep ramp at the back, followed by difficult passages of slow balances, he exposed the corps de ballet to more exacting demands than most of them had met before. During this and the next few seasons the Royal Ballet's corps reached a level of discipline, homogeneity, style and expressiveness which attracted admiration more than ever before. Others on the staff deserve credit for that, but a share in the achievement must have been Nureyev's with this *Bayadère* production.

His own contribution to the first-night performance was

unfortunately truncated when, whipping himself through the air in his first big solo, he realized that he was in danger of losing his balance and ran offstage prematurely rather than come a cropper. (I think it was probably during rehearsals for this work that one of the Royal Ballet staff pointed out how he could simplify one step and still look spectacular, to which he was reported as replying, "How can I work if I don't give myself something I can't do?") The accident produced evidence that some people were still willing to put every action of Nureyev's in the worst light. One American dance paper carried a factual report from its London correspondent and, on the same page, a gossip column paragraph alleging that he had "flounced off . . . in a fit of temperament," which was nonsense. Nureyev returned to dance the rest of that performance triumphantly and subsequently proved, at his best, unmatchable not only in the virtuoso solo, but also in the air of drama he brought to the ballet. It has remained, ever since, one of the Royal Ballet's most consistently popular works.

A week after the premiere came Fonteyn's annual RAD gala. Nureyev danced three roles, all of them for the first time on a London stage. He and Fonteyn performed the extracts from Bournonville's *La Sylphide* which they had already danced on tour. Kenneth MacMillan arranged a jaunty, jazzy solo for Nureyev, to a fantasia by Bach, which was given only on this one occasion. Nureyev also mounted the pas de deux *Diana and Acteon* for himself and Svetlana Beriosova, with whom he had already filmed it for television, first in the United States and then in London. In addition, he coached Anya Linden and Christopher Gable in the pas de deux from *The Flames of Paris*, which the Royal Ballet had learned, on a Soviet tour two years earlier, from its choreographer Vassili Vainonen.

A week later the Royal Ballet's new production of *Swan*

Lake opened at Covent Garden, directed by Robert Helpmann with much new choreography by Ashton and incorporating three dances composed by Nureyev: the polonaise
for the end of the first scene, the mazurka for the ballroom
scene, and a revised version of the solo for Prince Siegfried
which he had created for himself during his first season in
the West, now adopted for all the casts. Nureyev was due to
dance the first night of the new production but was
knocked down by a motor scooter in the street four days
earlier and had to withdraw, although, of course, he did later dance it often.

He was back in good time to mount the pas de six from
Laurencia for a television spectacular transmitted live from
Covent Garden in February, with Nadia Nerina and himself
in the central roles and the other parts played by some of
the Royal Ballet's most promising young dancers: Merle
Park, Antoinette Sibley, Gable and Graham Usher. Two
months later he took two roles in the Royal Ballet's program celebrating Shakespeare's quatercentenary. One was
the title part in Robert Helpmann's short, phantasmagoric
Hamlet, representing the character's death dream, set to
Tchaikovsky's fantasy overture in a surrealist decor by Les-
lie Hurry. This was an acting rather than a dancing role,
even if there did seem to be more steps in it at this revival.
Nureyev's other part was a creation in MacMillan's *Images
of Love*. In this uneven and short-lived sequence of dances
inspired by quotations from the sonnets, Nureyev was seen
as the "outsider" who, in one form or another, recurs in
most of MacMillan's ballets. He also took part in the one
episode where the dancing itself achieved a really striking
image, a pas de trois with Lynn Seymour and Gable based
on Sonnet 144, beginning "Two loves I have, of comfort and
despair. . . ." The ending of this, with Nureyev tugging at

the inert bodies of the other two, provided a choreographic metaphor pregnant and passionate enough to evoke Shakespeare's own imagery, but it needed the personalities of its original cast to bring it off; as soon as the dancers changed, it lost its startling urgency. Gable at that time was an impressively talented dancer whose own individual qualities were maturing rapidly by contact with Nureyev, and Seymour's sense of drama has always matched that of both these men.

Nureyev, however, had to leave *Images of Love* rather soon because he was committed to performances with Fonteyn in Stuttgart (where they danced another new version of *Swan Lake*, Cranko's production, which runs from an unexpected comic opening to an ending where the unrelieved nature of the tragedy is equally unusual) and then in Australia. On returning, they were due to dance two special performances with Western Theatre Ballet at the Bath Festival, but on the opening night Fonteyn's husband, Roberto Arias, was shot and severely injured in Panama. She danced that evening after being told he was out of danger. They gave the *Sylphide* extracts again, and a strange duet, called *Divertimento*, arranged for them by MacMillan to Béla Bartók's Sonata for solo violin, played onstage by Yehudi Menuhin. The choreography, in a groping, sinuously hesitating style, had hints of Orpheus leading Eurydice through limbo. Nureyev took to the unusual style with complete assurance, and if Fonteyn seemed less at home, that was probably for reasons the audience knew nothing of at the time. The dancers, in response to enthusiastic applause, even repeated the whole work, but the next morning Fonteyn flew to Panama, and it was never given again.

Her husband's arrival in Britain for hospital treatment also made Fonteyn miss the first performance, the following month, of Nureyev's first three-act production, *Raymonda*. This was commissioned by the Festival of Two Worlds at Spoleto and danced by the Royal Ballet's touring company. At the time, hardly anyone realized the extent of the task Nureyev had set himself in this production. It was taken for granted that he must be completely familiar with the work from his Leningrad days and merely had to reproduce it from memory, perhaps with some slight adaptations. In fact, he had danced in the male pas de quatre which is one of the highlights of the last act but had never played the lead. However, during his time as a student he had not only studied the standard repertory, role by role, with his teacher Pushkin, but had been assiduous in attending performances, with his eyes out on stalks for every detail. That was how he came to have the knowledge to mount works he had never danced, as well as those in which he had performed.

His task at Spoleto was complicated by a designer, chosen by the festival, who suddenly went off along a tangent of his own devising. Nureyev had specified the sort of scenery and costumes he had in mind to re-create the style of the late nineteenth century. But the designer, Beni Montresor, unilaterally decided that these "antiquated trappings of veils and embroidery" were incompatible with the artistic personalities of Fonteyn and Nureyev, who, he thought, must be given the opportunity "to project the human element, so rich and exceptional in these two artists." Fine aims, but wrong reasoning, because part of the talent of Fonteyn and Nureyev is to bring humanity to old styles, so that those are not just museum pieces.

Instead of a modern equivalent of the old style of setting, which would have given his production a context, Nureyev found himself working with a series of colored screens for background. Montresor's argument was that these would "strip away the tinsel" of romantic ballet "to bring out its essence, to present it in a fresher and more timely way." As Nureyev had already simplified the ballet's complicated plot, what was left looked, in these decors, almost like an abstract work. The ballet had been announced for the company's autumn tour, but it was decided that in this form it would not work, and after its festival performances the production was withdrawn.

For the Royal Ballet's young dancers, however, including Doreen Wells, who replaced Fonteyn in the title part until the latter arrived in time for the last performance, it was a stimulating experience. For Nureyev, the experience may have been more frustrating, but he was able to build on it with his subsequent productions of the same work. The surprising thing about the venture is that, for the first time, Nureyev was creating his own choreography on a large scale, to supplement and weld together the dances from Petipa's original production which he incorporated. However experienced he was—at the ripe old age of twenty-six!—as a dancer and in mounting other people's choreography, as a creator he was still a novice, but prepared to undergo his baptism in the conditions of a major festival to which other dancers and critics from many countries would come.

Less than three months later, he began the 1964–65 season with his second full-evening production. This was *Swan Lake*, at the Vienna State Opera, again with Fonteyn and himself as guest stars for the first performances, although several other casts went into the roles afterward. I asked Nureyev whether he had not found it daunting to undertake two major enterprises, *Raymonda* and this, so quickly one after the other. "I don't think they were really so close, were they?" he replied. "No, you are right. But there had been months of planning first with Georgiadis for *Swan Lake,* for instance, discussing all the details of how we would arrange things. I find that it always takes me just four weeks to mount a new production; that's the time they have all taken in preparation with the company and two weeks' rehearsal onstage."

I asked whether he was one of those choreographers who arrive at rehearsal with everything worked out in advance. "No. I have an idea of a certain effect I want, but we work it out in rehearsal. For a big corps de ballet number I might put down some notes on paper first, but even then I often change it."

The Vienna *Swan Lake* incorporated the traditional choreography by Ivanov for Act 2, the first lakeside scene, but the other three acts were newly set by Nureyev. One reason he has amended all the classics in his productions of them is that "Petipa created almost nothing for the male dancer. The pas de quatre in *Raymonda,* but that's about all." Also, he wants always to present the work from a definite point of view. Thus, in his *Swan Lake* the Prince became the focus on the grounds that the Swan is only a projection of him. But whatever changes he makes, he always keeps Petipa's basic structure "because it's so logical; you simply cannot get away from it."

Also, he thinks it important that whatever changes are made, the traditional versions should not be forgotten. When John Field was mounting *Swan Lake* at La Scala, Milan, in 1973, with Nureyev due to dance the opening performances, he told me, "I hope it is going to be very old-fashioned. I tried to encourage Field to keep all the old details, even to bring back the character of Benno, the prince's friend, who has been expelled from all other productions. I once saw the Petipa production for the peasant dance and waltz in Leningrad: Lopukhov revived it as faithfully as possible for the Maly Theater. I think it would be very interesting if it were possible to get a script of that; I remember it with lots of garlands. I think at least one production should try to preserve these things."

However, in 1964 changes were in the air. It is an odd thing that ballet revivals tend to go in waves. There were three major reworkings of *Swan Lake* within less than a year, and Nureyev danced in all of them. He and Cranko were more radical in their thinking than Helpmann. In particular, Nureyev (like Cranko before him) accepted the logic that, as Siegfried betrays the swan queen Odette when he mistakes Odile for her, there ought not to be a happy ending, even to the limited extent of the lovers' being reunited in death. This is a debatable point, arguably running counter to the implications of the music, but they each made sense of it. Both livened up the first act a great deal by introducing more dances. Cranko incorporated an eccentric element of surprise by making Siegfried start off with a practical joke, appearing first in disguise as a fortune-teller. Nureyev stuck to more traditional lines but invented a bravura dance for Siegfried and a group of friends. As in all his productions, he was concerned (among other considerations) to build up the leading male role, one of his reasons for mounting the classics being "to make opportunities for myself." But his changes were never arbitrary; they always tended to support a logical understanding of the style and shape of the ballet as a whole and to help bring it into focus by approaching it from a clear dramatic viewpoint.

There were difficulties during the mounting of *Swan Lake*. The Ballet of the Vienna Opera is a large company run on old-fashioned lines, where the dancers have life contracts like civil servants. That fact and the rather unadventurous artistic policy of previous years had led to the existence of a large group of dancers more advanced in years than in ability. Nureyev made no secret of his impatience with these, but he singled out some young dancers to share the leading parts, Michael Birkmeyer and Ully Wührer, both of them corps de ballet members without previous experience in leading roles, who enjoyed a big success as a result of his encouragement and coaching.

The production was filmed and thus remains on record, although with an adaptation of Nicholas Georgiadis' designs which does not satisfy the artist. The work proved immensely popular in Vienna, and this version was still being danced ten years later.

Back in London, Nureyev had another revival to mount for that year's RAD gala: the grand pas from the old ballet *Paquita*. This was a classical divertissement which Petipa had introduced into the ballet. Nureyev chose four promising young Royal Ballet dancers for the solos: Deanne Bergsma, Vyvyan Lorrayne, Monica Mason and Georgina Parkinson, all of whom he has danced with, helped and advised on subsequent occasions. They supported Fonteyn and himself in the leads, but the important ensemble dances were given to a group of students from the Royal Ballet School, who did reasonably well but, inevitably, within certain limits. This showpiece did not catch the enthusiasm of the London public at the time, although a later production by the Kirov Ballet was a big hit in London, and Nureyev's staging has been revived several times in Europe and America.

Shortly afterward Nureyev had to undergo an operation to remove his tonsils. While convalescing, he went for Christmas to Toronto, where his friends Lynn Seymour and Erik Bruhn were dancing as guests with the National Ballet of Canada. Bruhn was mounting *La Sylphide* for the company, and Nureyev attended rehearsals, just watching, although with the idea that he would like to dance the whole ballet one day. The chance came sooner and more abruptly than he expected, because Bruhn pulled a muscle, and once more Nureyev found himself propelled at short notice into a major role. Bruhn's injury was on January 1, but he managed to dance that night. A Canadian dancer, Earl Kraul, had already learned the role and went on the next night, but Nureyev took over on January 5. This capacity to learn a ballet in a few days (even quicker, sometimes, for a one-act ballet) has been crucial in his career. Without it, he could never have gone as he did from company to company, tackling new parts all the time. With a smaller repertory, his success in commercial terms and with the public would have been just as great, but he would have lacked the stimulus and satisfaction he has made for himself.

Tonsils were not the only thing troubling Nureyev that year. He has always suffered with his ankles. When he found out that I was born under the same sign of the zodiac as he, his first comment was: "So you have weak ankles, too," which I had to admit was true. I was surprised, not having known until then either that astrology was one of Nureyev's many interests or that we Pisceans are supposed to be especially liable to bad ankles. During 1965 Nureyev's ankles were causing him more difficulty than usual. In Canada he slipped on the ice. On his return to London (after dancing *The Corsair* with Fonteyn for President Johnson's inaugural gala in Washington), he landed heavily when jumping off a bus. He had to miss some performances but would not think of withdrawing from the first night of MacMillan's *Romeo and Juliet* at Covent Garden on February 9 or from the film made of that work later the same year, the *Daily Express* carried a big story under banner

headlines about how he had gone "crashing to the floor
. . . grimaced with pain and clutched his left ankle." After
massage, he went on dancing and smiling. There was a later
season, too, when he had hurt himself badly and was, in
fact, afraid that the injuries might be even more serious
than was obvious, but he carried on dancing in heavy ban-
dages. Except when it was physically impossible, his attitude has always been that a dancer's career was too short to
let little things like injury or pain keep him offstage. And,
as was the case with Romeo, some of his best performances
have been given in these conditions.

A short-lived revival of the Polovtsian dances from
Prince Igor, with Fokine's choreography mounted by Grigoriev, gave him his next new role at Covent Garden. His performance as the leading warrior had a taut ferocity but was
unable to transform a rather genteel ensemble. This production was first given at a gala, when the program also
included a repeat of the *Laurencia* pas de six. Subsequent
performances of *Prince Igor* introduced a change in the tick-
et-pricing system at Covent Garden. For some time, performances when Fonteyn danced had cost more than other
nights. From this time, enhanced rates applied also when
Nureyev danced, even if Fonteyn was not appearing.

This recognition of his effect on the box office did not
mean that Nureyev had become an uncontroversial figure.
There were some nasty comments in New York that summer because publicity for the Royal Ballet's season there
concentrated on him and Fonteyn, the two guest stars, but
it is difficult to see how anybody except the American impresario could be blamed for that. There was another flurry
of undeserved notoriety over an incident when Nureyev
was on a holiday in Monte Carlo after the tour. An Italian
photographer, Domenico Gatto, wanted to take pictures of

him beside a swimming pool, but Nureyev very reasonably refused to pose. The photographer shoved at him, and Nureyev fell in the water, whereupon his friends pushed the photographer in too, camera and all. Signor Gatto declared he would sue for compensation. Nureyev's only published comment was: "I don't want to talk about this stupid affair," but probably some people, reading the reports inattentively, thought of him afterward as the dancer who pushed a photographer into a swimming pool.

Not that he had much time to worry about such incidents. That autumn of 1965 he mounted a revised version of his *Raymonda* for the Australian Ballet. The company had come to Britain for the Commonwealth Festival and was offered a European tour on condition of having Fonteyn and Nureyev as guests. Its director, Peggy van Praagh, took the opportunity of mounting two new productions. She herself staged *Giselle,* and Nureyev was to produce *Don Quixote.* He actually taught it to the company, but then it was decided to put on *Raymonda* instead, partly because it offered a better role for Fonteyn. This time Nureyev's production was seen in several major cities. Ralph Koltai designed new settings, an experiment (which did not quite come off) in providing an illusion of old-fashioned solidity by modern means. The ballet stretched the dancers' abilities, but they mostly coped well. When the company was in Paris, Nureyev naturally turned up at the Théâtre des Champs-Élysées to see the Kirov Ballet, which appeared under the auspices of the same festival, and his casual arrival equally naturally caused a stir. When the production reached London, the opening night at the New Victoria (a cavernous theater generally used as a movie house) was made that year's RAD gala: Fonteyn had finally reached the point of being no longer able to gather together a fresh assembly of stars each year, and this was the last of her annual galas.

Part of the rehabilitated *Raymonda*, the celebratory dances from the last act, went back into the repertory of the Royal Ballet's touring company the following summer, with a further new decor by Barry Kay. During 1966 Nureyev also mounted three major new productions. One of them was his first work created from scratch. So far he had mounted new versions of old classics, and although that involved finding an individual interpretation of the work and sometimes creating large sections of new choreography, the basic structure of the work was there as a starting point. For *Tancredi*, created at the Vienna Opera in May, 1966, he had no such aid.

Hans Werner Henze had written a ballet score, *Tancred und Cantylene*, in the early 1950s to a libretto by Otto Herbst. It had one performance at Munich in 1952 with choreography by Victor Gsovsky and was then withdrawn by the composer. It was a completely revised version of this, sparse and airy in its orchestration and cut from about fifty minutes to half an hour, which was offered to Nureyev, complete with a new libretto by Peter Csobadi, a writer living in Berlin. In the event, Nureyev considerably amended the plot to suit his own conception of the work. It might have been more satisfactory for everyone if the ballet had been prepared wholly as a collaboration. Some spectators found themselves confused by the action that finally emerged, although that may have been partly because Nureyev chose to work through poetic allusion rather than in a specific narrative.

The hero, Tancredi, was born from a group of "life givers" and an *Urmutter* ("mother of all"). He met a romantic "first female image," who seemed to attract him in a chaste way, and a more blatantly seductive "second female image." Faced with the choice between sacred and profane love, spirit and flesh, Tancredi split himself into two with the aid of another character called his "second self." Their conflict led to death and a return to the womb. This plot was complicated by other characters including the seven reflections of Tancredi and seven mirror images of the first female image. (The distinction between *Reflektionen* and *Spiegelungen*, reflections and mirror images, was made in the cast list.)

Nureyev's program note said, "The conflicts within a man are demonstrated in scenes connected with the logic of poetry, rather than real action. Tancredi falls victim to his own desires and imagination." Although at the time the psychological content was declared obscure, audiences today, having grown used to a more indirect way of conveying meaning in dance, might not find such difficulty as people did in 1966. Even then, much of the dance invention was admired, especially the way Nureyev had shown off all the soloists. Apropos that, he told me, "When I did this work, everyone said I was interested only in myself, so I divided up the music carefully to give equal opportunity for all my cast, as well as myself." He also provided some vigorously athletic dances for the male ensemble.

The ballet had only four performances. Nureyev danced Tancredi at the first and last of them, May 18 and June 24, with Lisl Maar and Ully Wührer as the two female images. Karl Musil, one of the leading Viennese dancers, replaced Nureyev at the second performance, and the third was given to a cast of promising young dancers: Michael Birkmeyer, Lilly Scheuermann and Inge Kozna. At the end of the season, the erudite director Aurel Milloss left Vienna, and his successor, Vaslav Orlikovsky, dropped *Tancredi*, perhaps for fear that it would not be good box office without the choreographer in the title part. Nureyev's view is: "The public liked it, to judge by the applause. I am not sure the ballet was a success, but it was definitely not a failure from the public's point of view. And for myself, I wanted to find out whether I had a vocabulary to express myself in movement, and I was satisfied there was something there."

Nureyev had only one other new role that summer, the Messenger of Death in MacMillan's new production of *Song of the Earth* (an interpretation of Mahler's Song Cycle) at Covent Garden, which he played with expressive vividness, broodingly sinister, although without surpassing the two fine dancers who had already taken the role, Egon Madsen (for whom it was created) in Stuttgart and Anthony Dowell in London. Most of his time that year, after *Tancredi*, was taken up with two further full-evening productions. *The Sleeping Beauty*, first given at La Scala, Milan, in September, was a sumptuously heavy production, a complete surprise after the lightness of the Kirov version in which he had been brought up, but justified as a reflection of Tchaikovsky's music. *Don Quixote*, given at Vienna in December, was at the opposite extreme of Nureyev's range, a lighthearted comedy bearing much the same relationship to most long ballets as an operetta does to grand opera. With these two works (discussed in detail in a later chapter), Nureyev had entirely found himself as a producer. The conductor John Lanchbery, who was in Vienna to work with Nureyev on *Don Quixote*, adapting and reorchestrating Minkus' music, told me an example of how Nureyev used humor to get his own way at rehearsals. One of the more elderly members of the company was proving less than satisfactory, but it was difficult to complain because the dancers at Vienna have contracts which keep them on the books until the time comes to draw their pension. Nureyev called him over. "Your name?" he asked, and pretended to write it down, then offered the imaginary document to the dancer with the explanation "Your pension." After that, Nureyev had no trouble.

He might now have begun to seem a rather established figure, but his dancing came under criticism of a different sort from that in the early days. Over the next couple of years even those who admired his work found it distressingly uneven. There were too many bumpy landings, and his partnering did not always seem so helpful as it might have been. As always with someone prominently in the public eye, the reports were exaggerated, but they had a basis of truth. He could still at times give an absolutely stunning performance, but he might appear off form the next night.

Partly that was because any dancer must have some off nights; like an athlete, he cannot be always at the peak of his form. Also, Nureyev was at a difficult age. In the late twenties the muscles are less able than they were earlier to accomplish some physical feats, and he had not yet had time to acquire the craft that would enable him to overcome that by substituting other qualities. A further factor was that he was trying to do too much at once. Often rushing from one city to another with no time for rest, dancing, producing, he was straining too hard. Finally he got to grips with this, and it is characteristic that he solved the problem not by cutting down the number of his performances or the variety of places he went to, but by ordering them more methodically and eliminating other activities which interrupted them.

There was to be another American tour by the Royal Ballet in the summer of 1967, for which the French choreographer Roland Petit was commissioned to make a new work starring Fonteyn and Nureyev. His *Paradise Lost* did not last long in the repertory, but it did include some spectacular passages for Nureyev, including a tremendous run around and around the stage, at the end of which he disappeared from view by leaping between the lips of the huge portrait featured in Martial Raysse's pop-art backcloth. However, another Petit ballet, *Le Jeune Homme et la Mort*, filmed for television about this time, proved to suit Nureyev less well, not because he danced it badly (if anything, the steps looked more impressive when he danced them), but because the role had been so closely built around the very different personality of Jean Babilée. Nureyev seemed too spruce for the decadent romanticism of the theme invented by Jean Cocteau, and he was not helped by the decor having been unsuitably simplified.

The United States tour that year was enlivened, if that is the right word, by what the San Francisco *Chronicle* headlined as THE GREAT BALLET BUST. Some fans in that city urged Fonteyn to come after a performance one night to a party in the Haight-Ashbury district, at that time famous as the home of the hippies. She pressed Nureyev to accompany her, which he did unwillingly because he had another engagement. Soon after they arrived, the party was raided by the police in circumstances which made the whole affair look like a put-up job, although who could have fixed it and with what motive never became clear, so the whole thing may have been mere mischance. The two dancers were among eighteen people arrested on charges of disturbing the peace and visiting a place where narcotics and marijuana were being used. When I asked Nureyev how the pair of them managed to remain so calm in these circumstances, he told me it was simple. Neither of them smokes, so there could have been no question of suggesting that they were involved with drugs. Thanks to the presence of reporters and television cameras, every detail of the event was widely publicized, including the bailing out of the two dancers for $300 each by the Royal Ballet's manager, Vernon Clarke. Fonteyn, who had wanted to visit the hippie district from "curiosity, just plain curiosity," managed to look amused most of the time. Nureyev's comment on leaving was "What children you are," and he breathed on one overinquisitive camera lens to blur the image.

That autumn Nureyev danced for the first time another of the roles with which he has become particularly associated, the title part in Balanchine's *Apollo*; his debut was in a revival at Vienna. Next, *Paradise Lost* was mounted at the Paris Opéra with its original principals, and between the dress rehearsal and the premiere Nureyev flew to London to save the day for the Royal Ballet by dancing *Swan Lake* on the opening night of the new season since everyone else who might have done it was ill.

There followed another of Nureyev's full-length productions, a highly successful new interpretation of *The Nutcracker*, which he tried out first in Stockholm for the Royal Swedish Ballet. The premiere was on November 17, and the intention was that Nureyev would then immediately mount the work at Covent Garden in time for Christmas. However, Nicholas Georgiadis had been commissioned to produce more elaborate designs for the London production to replace Renzo Mongiardino's Stockholm decor. Georgiadis was busy also with a new *Aïda* for Covent Garden, so the London premiere of *The Nutcracker* was postponed until the end of February. It became, and has remained, one of the most popular works in the Royal Ballet's repertory.

The preparation of *The Nutcracker* threw light on an aspect of Nureyev's character unfamiliar to most people, the way he gets on with children. For *The Nutcracker* he announced that he wanted a large children's corps de ballet drawn from the junior section of the Royal Ballet School at Richmond. Students from the upper school, who work at Baron's Court in studios adjoining those of the company, are customarily used for certain roles at Covent Garden, such as the mice in *The Sleeping Beauty,* thus gaining some stage experience before graduation. However, to use the younger pupils was unprecedented, but as Barbara Fewster (now the school's principal) told me, "What Rudi wants, Rudi gets, so it was all arranged." She was at that time in charge of the classes used and was struck by the way young dancers, whose span of interest and attention was normally limited to short periods, went on working enthusiastically when Nureyev was rehearsing with them, long past their usual teatime.

About this same time came another example of Nureyev's refusal to be put off by illness. On the first night of Ashton's *Jazz Calendar* on January 9, 1968, he was due to dance the "Friday's child" sequence with Antoinette Sibley; earlier in the evening he was intended to dance *La Bayadère.* After the dress rehearsal of the new work he developed an acute attack of influenza and was ordered to bed. Michael Coleman was picked to take his place in *Bayadère,* with Donald MacLeary taking over in *Jazz Calendar.* When the audience arrived for the premiere, they found big notices displayed outside the theater announcing that, since Nureyev could not appear, they were entitled to a refund of the difference between ordinary seat prices and the special Nureyev prices. Some queued for their money straight away in the freezing snow; others decided to come back later.

At about seven thirty-five, only five minutes after the advertised starting time, the lights in the auditorium dimmed, and the house manager, John Collins, came in front of the curtain. It seemed that he must have some further stroke of doom to announce, but after a teasing preamble, he revealed that less than an hour earlier an unexpected figure had presented himself onstage: Nureyev, breathing heavily, running a temperature of 102° F, but insisting that he would dance the new ballet, although he could not attempt the strenuous *Bayadère*. The announcement caused such excitement that even the normally bland Mr. Collins referred to the guest star simply as Rudi and forgot to mention which role he would be playing. Incidentally, the box office still gave refunds to all who claimed them, with surprising cheerfulness, too. Dancers often refer to each other by punning nicknames: in the Royal Ballet, Nureyev is called by some people Randolph Neveroff.

When Ashton's *Birthday Offering* was revived later that season, Nureyev partnered Fonteyn in the pas de deux, accentuating the ardor of the duet where previous casts had emphasized its grandeur. Ashton also added a new solo for Nureyev into the sequence of display numbers. It gave the impression that he had worked on the principle of trying to establish how many steps could possibly be fitted into one dance, a challenge which the dancer met nimbly.

That summer Fonteyn and Nureyev went on two separate tours with the Royal Ballet: first to New York with the big company for a season at the Met, then with the smaller company to several festival centers in Europe. The latter brought frayed tempers on all sides because of the difficult conditions, and at Granada there was a major incident when Fonteyn was upset by photographers clicking away in the orchestra pit during a performance of *Giselle*. The tour impresario, Julian Braunsweg, had given them permission without consulting the ballerina. She stopped the performance, Nureyev gestured to the photographers to go, and the cast in some embarrassment left the stage until the offenders had been evicted and the show could resume. On a later tour with another company I saw Nureyev deal efficiently but unobtrusively with a photographer who had similarly worked his way right to the edge of the stage. As he passed close to the man while circling the stage, he muttered a couple of words which could not be heard where I sat in the front rows, although their purport was clear. When that had no effect, he waited and snapped his fingers before starting his next solo, whereupon attendants noticed what was wrong and quickly hustled the man away.

During that 1968 tour Nureyev danced another Ashton role, Oberon in *The Dream*. Having been created for Anthony Dowell's slight, elegant physique and cool personality, it was obviously a tricky part for Nureyev, although other dancers had already shown that the role would stand up to various interpretations. Clive Barnes saw the end of the tour, in Bilbao, and wrote, "I was told, by a most interesting selection of people, that Nureyev was not going to be right as Oberon in *The Dream*. In fact, on a tiny stage, and without trying overmuch, he happened to be the best Oberon I have ever seen." Unfortunately, he did not play the part again for many seasons, resuming it only in the fall of 1975.

There were two more creations by Petit for Nureyev during the following winter. First came *L'Estasi*, created at La Scala and given also at the Paris Opéra: a not very clear allegory about a man's journey through life, set to Scriabin's *Poem of Ecstasy*. The other new Petit work was *Pelleas and Melisande*, created for the Covent Garden gala on March 26, 1969, marking Fonteyn's thirty-five years on the stage.

More significant than either of those was Nureyev's appearance with the Dutch National Ballet in Rudi van Dantzig's *Monument for a Dead Boy.* This was Nureyev's first contact with a modern dance style, away from the classical ballet technique in which all his training and previous experience had been. He himself proposed the idea to the choreographer, who at first hardly believed it was seriously meant. The work had won some notoriety for the graphic way it depicted both heterosexual and homosexual activities, but these were not included for sensationalism, only as essential parts of a seriously intended whole. Inspired by the death of a young poet, the ballet showed, in a series of vivid dreamlike scenes, the crucial events of a tragic life.

Modern dance has been defined, by one of its keenest advocates, John Martin of the New York *Times,* as a point of view. The term is used to describe any of the forms of serious theatrical dancing which, during the twentieth century, have established themselves as an alternative to classical ballet. Although many of the early experiments were made in Germany, it is in the United States that the art has chiefly flourished. Martha Graham, the most celebrated of contemporary exponents, codified a technique which could be taught to students in the same way as classical ballet is taught, but this was drawn empirically from the needs of her own choreography, and a feature of modern dance is that each major choreographer develops his own special kind of movement, whereas in ballet the choreographers are mainly concerned to make new patterns or meanings from the traditional steps.

The role in *Monument* marked a further widening of Nureyev's already impressive range. It was not unprecedented for dancers to tackle both classical and modern dance styles, and there were even some small companies which had adopted a policy of presenting a mixed repertory. But for someone of Nureyev's eminence in either tradition to involve himself in this was new and helped make the practice acceptable to the point that even the Royal Ballet was later prepared to take modern dance works into its repertory. Nureyev's pioneering in this respect gave fresh evidence of three aspects of his work and character: first, the fact that he had always wanted to avoid being typecast and was anxious to try as many different types of role as possible; secondly, his responsiveness to new trends in the arts while holding very firmly to the old classical tradition which provided his roots; thirdly, his courage in being prepared to try something new and be judged by the highest standards. In *Monument*, for instance, it was obvious that he would be compared with Toer van Schayk, who usually took the role. Van Schayk, a strong dancer in this style, had the advantage of having worked with the choreographer in the preparation of the ballet, actually designing it as well as dancing the lead at the first performance and ever since.

Although branching out into new styles, Nureyev did not neglect the old ones. When he first danced *Monument*, on Christmas Day, 1968, he insisted on dancing *The Nutcracker* pas de deux in the same program so that audiences could see him in the manner they expected, as well as in something unfamiliar. Almost a year later, when he danced *Monument* in London during the Dutch National Ballet's first season at Sadler's Wells, he took the opportunity also to be seen as Apollo, a classical role he had not previously played in London. He holds that dancing the classics regularly keeps a dancer in form, and between those two seasons with *Monument* his activities had included new versions of two familiar ballets. At Covent Garden he appeared in the new production of *The Sleeping Beauty* for which

Solo from
The Corsair

With Rosella Hightower
in *Fantaisie* (1961)

With Sonia Arova, Rosell
Hightower and Erik Bruhn i
Toccata and Fugue (1961)

Conducting a rehearsal in R
sella Hightower's studio a
Cannes (1961)

Amid the setting for the Cuevas Ballet's *Sleeping Beauty*, June, 1961

Kirov Ballet rehearsals in Paris (1961): *La Bayadère* and *The Sleeping Beauty*

Directing the film of
Don Quixote with
the Australian Ballet
and a rehearsal of
The Sleeping Beauty
with the National
Ballet of Canada
(both 1972)

As Solar in *La Bayadère* with Margot Fonteyn

First Meeting

In the Country

With Margot Fonteyn

in *Marguerite and Armand*

Marguerite's Death

Solo in *Romeo and Juliet,*
Act 2

As Des Grieux in *Manon*
(1975)

With Margot Fonteyn after the pas de deux in *The Sleeping Beauty*, Act 3

Solo in *The Sleeping Beauty*, Act 3 (Royal Ballet's 1969 production)

Solo in *The Sleeping Beauty,*
Act 2 (his production for National Ballet of Canada)

Portrait in a dressing-room
mirror (about 1961)

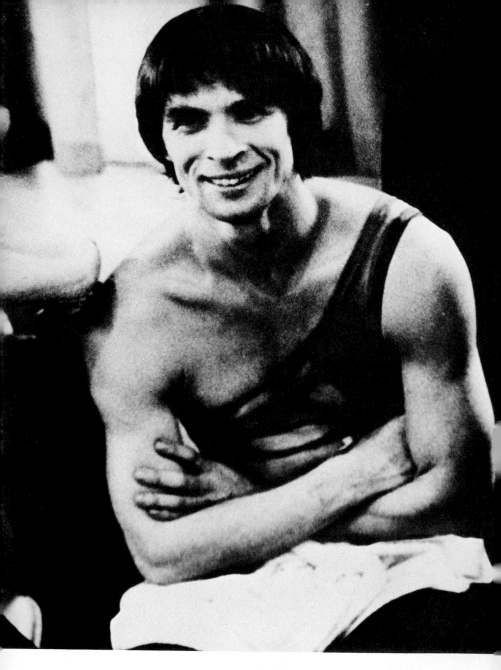

Dressing-room portrait in costume for *The Ropes of Time* (1970)

Solo in *Giselle*, Act 2, with the National Ballet of Canada

With Margot Fonteyn in *Giselle*, Act 2 (Royal Ballet)

Directing *The Nutcracker* in Stockholm (1967)

With Merle Park in *The Nutcracker,* Act 2 (Royal Ballet)

In Maurice Béjart's *Le Sacre du Printemps* (1971)

With Lucette Aldous in *Don Quixote,* Act 3 (Australian Ballet, 1973)

arsing *Don Quixote*
Frances Croese as Ki-
ather (1973)

As Basilio in *Don Quixote*, Act 1

With Linda Yourth, Merle Park and Lisa Bradley in *Apollo* (New York, 1974)

Beginning of Scene 2 of *Apollo*

With Jerome Robbins during rehearsal of *Dances at a Gathering* (1970)

With Laura Connor and Ann Jenner in *Dances at a Gathering*

Ashton had created an extra solo and pas de deux, both very dreamily romantic in mood. At the Paris Opéra he danced the *Swan Lake* that had been produced by the Russian choreographer Vladimir Bourmeister, also with many different dances.

Van Dantzig created Nureyev's next new role specially for him. That was in *The Ropes of Time,* given by the Royal Ballet in March, 1970. The audience at the Royal Opera House regarded it as decidedly avant-garde; it even introduced *musique concrète* for the first time to that auditorium. Again he was playing the traveler through life, accompanied by love and death, but this time the choreography, aided by the moving sculptures which Van Schayk had created for the setting, conveyed the idea in more unusual and striking terms. There was also an implication, in the imagery of the dances, of a theme that must be relevant to any reigning champion in sport or the arts: the struggle to retain mastery in spite of the challenges of youthful rivals and the depredations of time.

There could hardly have been a more vivid contrast, therefore, than the revival for the Australian Ballet, later that same month, of *Don Quixote,* the ballet the company had nearly presented four years earlier. Nureyev, who went out to dance it himself, revised the production from what he had already done in Vienna, changing the order of scenes in the quest for a smoother, more logical flow. Lucette Aldous, at that time still a ballerina of the Royal Ballet, although she later joined the Australians permanently, danced Kitri, and Robert Helpmann played the title part.

In July Nureyev was back in London for a great occasion, the special performance arranged by staff and dancers of the Royal Ballet at Covent Garden to mark Ashton's retirement as their director. A selection of dances representing all periods of his career, many of them having been absent from the repertory for many years, was rehearsed in secret. It was suggested that Nureyev might dance the *Poème tragique* which Ashton had created for his London debut, but with such a long gap since its only performance, he could no longer remember it. Instead, he took two other Ashton roles for the first time. One was the leading man in *Les Rendezvous,* a lighthearted mixture of exuberance and romance. The part had been made in 1933 for the Polish virtuoso Stanislas Idzikovski. During rehearsals Helpmann (who was master of ceremonies for the gala and had taken a supporting part in the original production of *Rendezvous*) taught Nureyev a fiendish complication of one step in the solo which had been omitted by recent Royal Ballet casts; no wonder that Nureyev's comment later was: "I could hardly feel my legs when I came offstage." His other part at the Ashton gala was the poet searching for his elusive ideal beloved in the ballroom scene from *Apparitions,* partnering Fonteyn in the role she had originally danced with Helpmann—whose comment, coming on to announce the next item, was "My interpretation was *very* different." That got a big laugh, partly because of Helpmann's wryly sardonic manner, but probably also because nobody had realized, until Nureyev performed it, giving full value to every step, how much dancing there was in what had seemed mainly a mimed role.

Nureyev's admiration for Ashton has always been great, but he told me that he had never realized, from reading about them, just how good Ashton's earliest ballets had been. When the entire cast, waltzing to music from *A Wedding Bouquet,* turned to the choreographer and bowed at the end of the evening, nobody inclined his back lower or more graciously than Nureyev.

That was the summer when one of Nureyev's near contemporaries, Natalia Makarova, abruptly left the Kirov Ballet during a London season at the Royal Festival Hall. The circumstances were very different from those in which he had left nine years earlier. She had a secure position in the company, with no danger of being relegated for dissenting from the party line on artistic matters. It was suggested that emotional or romantic factors had provided part of her motive, but it never became clear that there was any better foundation for this story than for baseless attempts to hint something similar of him at the time of his departure. Certainly her chief motive, like his, was a wish for greater freedom and variety of artistic choice. As soon as the news broke of Makarova's disappearance from her hotel, people likely to know Nureyev were deluged with telephone calls from reporters and news agencies anxious to associate him with the event. Fortunately, he was not in Britain at the time, so all attempts were frustrated. In fact, the first he heard of it was a telephone call from friends in London after Makarova had already gone into hiding.

Nureyev was busy that summer spending what should have been his vacation in making a television film in France, which later formed the basis of the bigger film *I Am a Dancer*. Next came a major new role at Covent Garden in the British premiere of Jerome Robbins' *Dances at a Gathering*. Although the work consisted, formally, just of a sequence of mainly plotless dances to Chopin piano music, its scope (lasting just over an hour), the variety of moods and the hints of relationships among the ten members of the cast have made it one of the most admired and influential ballets of recent years. If Nureyev's part, dancing the first and last solos, as well as several other entries, gave him special prominence, he remained the first among equals in that original Royal Ballet cast, and he relished the chance to be seen dancing in that way, entirely as one of the company rather than as a guest star. The sense of friendship among all the dancers was one of the most attractive features of this fine ballet.

That was Nureyev's first appearance in a ballet by Robbins, and the following winter brought his first experience also of two other choreographers. The first was Paul Taylor, the American modern dancer, who agreed to create a short work for Nureyev to dance on television in New York. Taylor adapted a piece he was already working on, *Big Bertha*, a gripping horror-comic dance about a figure on a mechanical organ (Bettie de Jong) who comes to life and overcomes unsuspecting victims. In the stage version which Taylor completed later for his company, she destroys a whole family, but on television Nureyev alone fell under her spell and was eventually transformed into an apparently mechanical figure like herself.

Maurice Béjart was the other choreographer to create a ballet specially for Nureyev that season, a duet for two men to Mahler's *Lieder eines fahrenden Gesellen*. Paolo Bortoluzzi, one of the stars of Béjart's Ballet du XXme Siècle, was the other dancer, who appeared to represent the hopes and fears of the traveler through life played by Nureyev. The work was first given in a special week of performances in the huge auditorium of the Forest Nationale, Brussels, which seats 5,800 and was sold out every performance. For this season Nureyev also learned and danced the leading male part in Béjart's version of *The Rite of Spring*, which has two sacrificial victims, a man and a woman. It is a role calling for bold emotional expression, which Nureyev provided with the appearance of fierce commitment.

These new roles by no means exhausted Nureyev's activities, notable among which was a coast-to-coast tour of the United States and Canada with the Australian Ballet. He joined the company in Los Angeles the day after Christmas, and the tour, which included two weeks at the New York City Center, ended in Boston ten weeks later. During that time he danced almost every performance, either the full-evening *Don Quixote* or a new divertissement from *Raymonda* comprising most of the final act of his former production and some dances from earlier in the ballet. Far from being worried about appearing so often, he positively enjoyed it. He told me, "I danced six nights a week, twice on Saturdays—and each week one of the Saturday performances was the best of the week: sometimes the matinee, sometimes the evening. I dance best when I am tired. Then I know what I am doing; my muscles just work my way."

This pleased audiences but annoyed some of the Australian dancers. When the tour was announced, some leading members of the company declared that they were resigning in protest at "the lack of harmony between all of us and the management. No one begrudges the presence of Nureyev. He is probably the greatest dancer in the world . . . but it would also be marvelous performing as a company and not as a background for Nureyev." The protest might have carried more weight but for the fact that several of the dancers concerned had in fact put in their resignations sometime earlier, for other stated motives. Also, it was quite obvious that without Nureyev the company would not have been invited to the United States. Thanks to his presence, they had the chance to be seen in New York and several major cities, dancing other works from their repertory, as well as his productions.

There was some more brouhaha about this tour when comments were published about Nureyev's tights, thought by some observers to be excessively transparent. Scathingly, Robert Helpmann (joint director of the company) pointed out that what audiences could see underneath was not flesh but another pair of tights worn ready for a quick costume change.

Two other companies found themselves extra engagements that season thanks to Nureyev. The Marseilles Ballet had the chance to take its production of *The Sleeping Beauty* to the huge Palais des Sports in Paris with him as guest, and a virtually unknown company from Buffalo, the Niagara Frontier Ballet, was offered a European tour with him and other guests. Renamed the American Classical Ballet for the occasion, the company was mainly young and inexperienced, but had received good basic training and coaching from its director, Kathleen Crofton, and from Bronislava Nijinska (Nijinsky's sister), who had mounted several productions. The main attraction of the tour for Nureyev was the chance to dance James in *La Sylphide*, a particularly rewarding (and demanding) part. Since he first learned it in Canada, he had given a few performances at the Rome Opera House but had not been seen very widely in the role.

Several other principal dancers had been engaged for the tour, including the young ballerinas Liliana Cosi and Eva Evdokimova, who both danced the title part in *La Sylphide*, but the posters made it clear that Nureyev's presence was the big selling point, with a cheerfully smiling photograph of him and the slogan "The most famous male dancer in the world." Unfortunately, that led to trouble at one performance. The program on which he danced James, a big role which kept him onstage for most of the ballet's two acts, alternated with another consisting of three one-act productions and a pas de deux. On the night I saw this program in a big hall outside Düsseldorf, Nureyev had just flown from London (where he was fitting in some performances with the Royal Ballet between his touring dates) and was cast to dance only in *Aurora's Wedding*—the last act of *The Sleeping Beauty*. In this, he was not required to appear until near the end, to dance the main pas de deux, with solos and a coda, and make an entry in the finale. The audience cheered each of his appearances, but at the end of the evening, thinking they had not seen enough of the star to justify the high price of tickets, many of them stood up and booed. Nureyev reacted to this rather charmingly by treating the boos as if they had been applause (and of course, many people were still applauding). He brought forward Cosi, who had danced Aurora, and presented her to the audience; he took a bow himself; he made the whole company join in. Not the slightest sign of any upset feelings was allowed to show. But when he went backstage afterward, his first action was to remark that when this program was given in other towns, he would also dance a pas de deux earlier in the evening.

That resolve was almost broken by force of circumstances at the end of the tour when the company gave a special gala at Madrid in aid of Unicef. Nureyev pulled a muscle in his left leg, and in spite of treatment, he was in agony. Even so, he insisted that he must make an appearance at the gala to avoid upsetting the audience and said he would dance in *Aurora's Wedding* since that was the last on the program and would give him at least some chance of recovering before he had to go on. However, the announcement (made, it seems, far too bluntly) that Cyril Atanassoff, one of the stars of the Paris Opéra, would replace him in the *Flower Festival at Genzano* pas de deux brought shouting and screaming. This continued even when the curtain went up, and it soon became impossible for the dancers to continue. The curtain was lowered again, and now it was announced that Nureyev was injured but in spite of that would be appearing later in the program. Still the pandemonium continued, and Nureyev said he would dance *Flower Festival.* When they saw for themselves that his leg was bandaged, the audience fell silent, and at the end they cheered, although in his injured state Nureyev can scarcely have danced the difficult and delicate choreography well. Later in the evening, still in agony, Nureyev also danced the *Aurora's Wedding* pas de deux; but Julian Braunsweg, the impresario for the tour, recorded that when he congratulated Nureyev on his heroism, he got the reply "Never again."

In spite of this, Nureyev was back after only a short break for another exceptionally busy season. With the Royal Ballet he had new roles, one at the beginning and one at the end of the season, in the works of yet another choreographer of the new wave, Glen Tetley. His own training and background having been in several different styles, Tetley took elements from all of them to achieve his own kind of theatricality. Nureyev's first Tetley role was the central male part in *Field Figures,* a ballet in which the choreographer had (he wrote) taken as his starting point "the carefully judged distances we all unconsciously permit between ourselves and other people, and the instinctive guarding of territory about us that is part of our animal heritage." Inspired by that idea, the movement explored "the transitions between movements, rather than the fixed, brilliant positions usual in classical ballet," and concepts such as that "balance is a constant state as opposed to a heart-stopping verticality; above all to emphasize continuity." The central figure has a comparatively static role as the quiet center of the action, with the more brilliant moments given to others. Nureyev provided a strong focus and brought out more vividly than others had done the animal imagery which Tetley had woven into the action.

That role had been created the previous year for another dancer, but Nureyev was one of the cast of eight on whom Tetley devised his *Laborintus*, an immensely complex work with a sung and spoken text by Edoardo Sanguinetti, music by Luciano Berio and elaborate designs by Rouben Ter-Arutunian. It expressed a very modern view of life as a descent into inferno. Nureyev's role included a dance with Lynn Seymour in which she repeatedly hurled herself into his embrace and was held in twisted sculptural attitudes, another duet with Deanne Bergsma containing a canon of broad leaps to the side for both dancers and a solo in which a circuit of fast whirling leaps around the stage was given a very different weight from the usual classical manège.

Another new role at Covent Garden, the Red Knight in *Checkmate*, suited him less well: a pity, because this was the first time he had danced in one of Ninette de Valois' ballets. He had, in fact, asked if he could dance Satan in her *Job* (that and the title role in *The Rake's Progress* are among the parts he still covets), but *Checkmate* was chosen to honor the eightieth birthday of its composer, Sir Arthur Bliss. Looking unhappy in the high headdress—generally he tries to avoid wearing even a wig on stage—he gave the appearance of finding difficulty in adjusting his Kirov-trained conception of a mazurka to the choreographer's treatment of that rhythm in the main solo. He had far more success in another Robbins ballet, the Royal Ballet's new production of *Afternoon of a Faun*, where his sensuous quality of movement and dramatic flair had full scope. In addition, MacMillan made a comic duet, *Sideshow*, combining virtuoso steps and slapstick jokes, for him and Seymour to dance on the opening night of the Royal Ballet's New York season, which ran from late April until early June.

That made a total of five new parts during the 1971–72 season with the Royal Ballet alone. In addition, he played a season in Mexico City with Paul Taylor's company, dancing two of Taylor's own roles, in the limpid, lyrical *Aureole* and the comic *Book of Beasts*. Although they had both been built on Taylor's very different physique and personality, Nureyev was keen straightaway to be seen in these parts by audiences with a more knowledgeable background. He told me at the time that since he had not previously danced in Mexico, he feared that people were expecting to see him in the classical repertory and were not ready to see him in modern works. He said he would like to dance these new roles in London or New York, and he did later go to a great deal of trouble to ensure a London season for the Taylor company, during which he appeared as guest. Later still, while working in Paris, he flew to New York for one night to take part in one of Taylor's seasons there.

Also that winter of 1971–72 he went to Zurich to stage, and dance in, a completely reworked version of *Raymonda*, changing the action to make it all reveal the heroine's attitude toward her forthcoming marriage and adding several more dances to music he had previously omitted. Among other things, he told me, he thought it would be interesting to show the hero, Jean de Brienne, "as rather colorless at first. Then Raymonda thinks, 'If only he were a little more exciting' and dreams up this other character as a rival." From the time of the ballet's composition in 1898, the plot had never really made much sense, but with this interpretation it did at last hang together.

An incident on the first night of that production offers an

illustration of the remarkable way in which Nureyev's memory can work. Probably because he had so many other responsibilities to worry about, when he came to dance the new solo which he had created for himself, he found that it had slipped from his mind. But he could remember how it ended, so in his mind's eye he worked backward from the ending. Meanwhile, to cover the gap, he allowed his muscles to improvise movements in time with the music. When he came to the point where the music he was actually hearing coincided with the mental image, he knew that he could go on from there with the intended version. The covering up was so well done that it passed unnoticed by the audience, except that a friend of Nureyev's had observed his eyes glaze over while he was concentrating on the inward image and asked him afterward why that had been.

Between all these and other more routine engagements, much of Nureyev's time was taken up with the film *I Am a Dancer*, for which extra sequences had to be shot and the ones taken over from the original television film had to be reworked. He had many ideas about what should and should not be done and was disappointed with the result because it did not meet his expectations or his standards. Even so, the finished version was a great deal better than the first rough cut which I had the opportunity of seeing, and the improvements were mainly the result of his suggestions. Incidentally, Nureyev was pressed to allow his name to be used in the title of the film but refused on the grounds that to do so would be insulting to Fonteyn, who was also prominently featured, and he refused to hear of any more flamboyant title than the one eventually chosen. When he was persuaded to be interviewed by Terry Coleman for the *Guardian* as part of the advance publicity, he characteristically said what he thought was wrong with the film; this was not a cunning scheme to stir up more interest, but sheer honesty.

Later that year he again found himself before the cameras, when he mounted his production of *The Sleeping Beauty* for the National Ballet of Canada, and a shortened version (ninety minutes compared with more than two hours of actual performing time onstage) was filmed by a Canadian television company. This also disappointed him and confirmed him in the decision he had already made, to take personal responsibility for directing *Don Quixote* when it was filmed soon afterward with the Australian Ballet.

In addition to the *Beauty*, he danced *Swan Lake* and *La Sylphide* on tour with the Canadian Ballet in autumn, 1972, and the following spring, besides taking the title part in *The Moor's Pavane*, a four-character work based on the main characters of *Othello*. This was mounted for them that autumn by its choreographer, José Limón, shortly before his sudden death.

Within a few days of his first appearance as the Moor, Nureyev was on his way to Australia for the *Don Quixote* film. Before shooting began, the ballet was given a week's run at Sydney with the cast who were to appear in the film: Aldous (by now permanently with the Australian Ballet) and Nureyev in the leads, with Helpmann miming the title role. The whole film was then shot within four weeks in a large aircraft hangar outside Melbourne. Geoffrey Unsworth was director of photography; Nureyev and Helpmann were named as joint directors, but Nureyev, as the choreographer and as an assiduous filmgoer, not surprisingly took the more active part. On returning to Britain, Nureyev had a film editor staying in his home at Richmond and working there. That enabled the dancer to discuss with him each morning the next batch of work. If possible, Nureyev would rush home in the afternoon after class and rehearsal; then there would be a further working session in the evening or even late at night after his performance at Covent Garden. In spite of this grueling schedule, Nureyev had to leave for the second lap of his Canadian tour before the film was finished, so that the sound was added in his absence. "I shall know next time," he told me, "it's not enough to lay your own eggs; you have to hatch them, too." As usual, he was not himself content with the finished product, seeing all the small faults which others disregarded because they were looking at the large virtues. Many people, I think, would rate the result as the best film yet made of a full-length stage ballet, and it is startling to realize that a great part of it was accomplished in what might realistically be called his spare time from everyday activities.

During the winter of 1972–73 Nureyev also took part in a special program at the Paris Opéra in homage to Serge Diaghilev, whose centenary had fallen a few months earlier. He danced three ballets on the one program: *Les Sylphides, Apollo* and *Petrushka.* Returning to this last role after a long gap, he had first worked intensively on it in Holland with Rudi van Dantzig and Toer van Schayk for some performances with the Dutch National Ballet, and he warmly acknowledges their help in bringing it properly into focus. His performance now became a revelation of the real merits of what had seemed a mere relic of the past. On the nights when Nureyev did not appear in this Paris program, his roles were shared among two or sometimes three French dancers.

Back in London, he learned the title role in Balanchine's *Prodigal Son* and danced the premiere of the Royal Ballet's production before going to America for the second leg of his tour with the Canadian Ballet. Taking advantage of a brief gap in the tour schedule, just before the company appeared in New York, Nureyev went off to dance four performances (two matinees and two evenings) with an obscure regional company, the Wisconsin Ballet, in Madison and Milwaukee. What tempted him was the chance of dancing another of those extremely varied programs he so much enjoys: this time *Les Sylphides, Apollo* and *The Moor's Pavane,* with the added attraction that it was the first time he had danced *Apollo* in North America. After this, unfortunately, he again hurt his leg during the Canadian Ballet's New York run. Without him, their impresario canceled the Washington engagement that was to follow.

Nureyev was still troubled by the injury when he returned to London, but that did not stop him from giving all his scheduled performances during the Royal Ballet's spring season at the London Coliseum. When the company returned to its usual home at Covent Garden in June, he was cast to open the season dancing *The Sleeping Beauty* with Makarova. They gave three performances of this and three of *Romeo and Juliet.* It was the first time he had partnered her onstage; although they were in the Kirov Ballet together (she was graduated one year after him), he had spent much of his time partnering the senior ballerinas and within his own age group was generally paired with Alla Sizova. They had made one television appearance together soon after she left the Kirov, and the fact that they were graduates of the same school must have presented an irresistible temptation for putting them together. But both had changed a great deal since their schooldays and early youth, and their individual performances proved not to match very well.

They were also engaged to dance together in Paris that

summer of 1973, but first Nureyev danced several performances in London with Paul Taylor's company. Taylor was
on a European tour but without a London engagement; Sadler's Wells Theatre was free for a convenient week, and a
London manager offered to present the company, provided
that Nureyev would appear as guest. He not only agreed
with enthusiasm but rearranged all his schedules to make it
practicable, then added extra performances to the ones for
which he had originally been announced. Again the attraction was partly the possibility of being seen in unfamiliar
roles, partly the chance to work once more with a choreographer he much admired.

Arriving in Paris after this, Nureyev found a less happy
situation. The Paris Opéra Ballet was to give thirteen performances of *Swan Lake* on an open-air stage erected in one
of the courtyards of the Louvre. The first night, on Bastille
Day, was a free performance for the people of Paris. Nureyev was to dance every performance, but three dancers
were to take turns in the ballerina role: Noëlla Pontois and
Ghislaine Thesmar, two of the company's own stars, and
Makarova as guest. Unfortunately, the weather was not
what would be expected in Paris at the height of summer. It
was cold, windy and sometimes wet. Two performances
were rained out. At others the corps de ballet of swans wore
warm leotards under their ıtus, and Nureyev carefully
wrapped a cloak around his legs to keep his muscles warm
when he had to sit on a throne waiting for the time to
dance.

These circumstances were not such as to encourage happy feelings, and on top of her other troubles Makarova
slipped and fell. At her first performance, in consequence,
she omitted her solo and the coda from the pas de deux in
Act 3. Her next performance was complete, but the one af-

ter that was again truncated, which caused some unfavorable remarks by other dancers and voluble protests from the audience. Makarova then announced that she was not well enough to dance her remaining performances, which were therefore shared between the two French ballerinas.

All would have been well if she had not then made some rash comments to a reporter in San Francisco. Nureyev, she was quoted as saying, had been terribly jealous when he realized that the crowds had come to see her, not him. That was a strange assumption on her part since all 6,500 seats were sold out for every performance, whether she was dancing or not. She also declared, implausibly, that he only liked appearing with young dancers who would do what he told them, and added that "things are difficult for a man who is thirty-five." These tendentious comments were widely reported, but the subject of them refrained, as is his habit, from any public comment, and it is likely that the publicity reflected more harshly on Makarova herself.

Nureyev's only intervention in the season's difficulties was quietly transacted. On some nights the corps de ballet held a meeting to decide whether conditions were too bad to perform. Nureyev went to the tent which served as their dressing room and made a simple request: "If you decide not to dance, will you please make up your minds by eight thirty because the good movie starts then. By nine o'clock it's no longer interesting."

If dancing is, in fact, more difficult for a man of thirty-five, Nureyev did not let the disadvantage show. Certainly his dancing is very different nowadays from what it was ten or twelve years earlier. There are some feats of athletic virtuosity which only a young body can achieve, in dancing as in sport. But if Nureyev today no longer hovers in the air as his younger self once did, he has other qualities which he had not then developed. Young Nureyev was a more sensational dancer; Nureyev now is a better dancer. And he remains as active as ever.

Half of what should have been his summer holiday in 1973, after that Paris *Swan Lake* and a couple of performances at Covent Garden, was spent touring Israel with the Royal Ballet's smaller company because "it's such an interesting repertory." On return to London, via Milan for some performances there, he had another role to learn, in *Agon*, one of Balanchine's ballets in which he had first expressed a keen interest eleven years earlier. Then there were performances in Copenhagen (another of his favorite mixed programs: *Apollo, Aureole, The Moor's Pavane—*and *La Sylphide*), followed by some in Oslo, where he mounted the last act of *Raymonda*. After that, he had to revive his *Nutcracker* for the Royal Ballet and undertook extensive changes in the choreography, also dancing not just his own scheduled performances, but Anthony Dowell's, too, when the latter hurt himself. Next, he went to Milan for a run of *Swan Lake,* then to Canada again for another tour with the National Ballet there. And even that hectic itinerary is a gross simplification. For instance, while dancing and rehearsing in London, he flew off for a couple of gala performances in Monte Carlo and again for one in Versailles. (I have made no attempt to record all his multifarious engagements of this sort or the many engagements with major companies when he was simply repeating his standard repertory, but you must imagine a constant series of such activities as a background to all the new developments.) He flew from London to New York for one day to attend the charity premiere of the *Don Quixote* film there, because the organizers wanted his presence to help sell tickets, and he flew similarly from Milan to London for the

British first night, which was devoted to raising funds for the Australian Ballet. Having five days to spare during his Italian engagement, he returned to London to learn the role of Colas in Ashton's *La Fille mal gardée,* ready to make his debut in the part during the Royal Ballet's New York season in the spring, and at the same time he sat in on early rehearsals of MacMillan's *Manon* so that he could learn the part of Des Grieux more quickly when his turn came to dance it, also in New York.

As soon as he got to Toronto, to join the Canadian National Ballet, he had another new role to learn, the title part in *Don Juan* by yet another young choreographer whose work he was tackling for the first time, John Neumeier, an American who has spent most of his career in Germany. The ballet, set to Gluck's music with some interpolations from a requiem mass by Tomás Luis de Victoria, had already been given by the Frankfurt Ballet while Neumeier was director there, and the choreographer started teaching it to the Canadian dancers before Nureyev arrived. He told me that he was alarmed because people kept saying to him that "Rudolf will not like this or that," particularly about some of the difficult lifts in the duets, holding the ballerina out at his side. When the guest star arrived, he watched a run-through of what had been set, and Neumeier braced himself to explain that he would prefer not to make any changes in his choreography but would entirely understand if Nureyev preferred not to dance the role. "Why not? I'm strong," came the answer. The hero is shown as an elegant creature, too bored with the ease of his conquests to enjoy them, an intellectual rather than a man of action (his servant is the real lecher); when he falls in love with a woman who mysteriously appears to him, he discovers too late that she is the angel of death. He has a solo danced to a reading from Max Frisch's reflections on the true nature of Don Juan. Not at all Nureyev's usual kind of role, but one in which his performance was much admired.

Neumeier told me that for him "Nureyev is the ideal Don Juan, but when working with him I was embarrassed at times because the character as I conceived it is like his own. I would explain, 'When you come into a room, you are aware of everybody looking at you,' or, 'Sometimes you do something because people expect it of you,' and I realized that was too close to the truth."

The Canadian Ballet's 1974 spring tour ended at the Metropolitan Opera House on May 5, and on May 7 the Royal Ballet opened a New York season in the same theater. Nureyev went straight from one company to the other. That season included his first New York performance of Balanchine's *Apollo,* a ballet in which his interpretation, revealing the character and drama implicit in the choreography, is far removed from the abstract way the choreographer nowadays likes the role played in his own company, the New York City Ballet. But the cogency and conviction of his reading compelled acceptance.

There was no need for him to apply any fresh interpretation to Ashton's version of *La Fille mal gardée;* the comedy and romance of the plot, lovers united in spite of parental opposition, is clearly defined in the choreography. But he did find a lot of convincing detail, emphasizing the bucolic side of the work, and what was particularly attractive about his playing in this ballet was that it permitted him to show the simple, unforced charm and good humor which are part of his real nature but rarely revealed onstage.

By contrast, the part of Des Grieux presented difficulties, because although individual scenes of *Manon* were striking, the development of the plot was not strong in logic.

115

Nureyev brought touches of liveliness to the character by reacting to every immediate stimulus: a realization, for instance, that a passing rat catcher would stink or that the hero would feel self-conscious and stiffly uncomfortable when he first put on his new finery. The soft gentleness of his dancing in the more lyrical solos was a reminder that he had himself pioneered this kind of choreography for men in the *Swan Lake* solo he created early in his career, but in other episodes he danced with an angry vehemence appropriate to the plot.

That summer of 1974 saw the logical development of Nureyev's interest in a program of short contrasting works, with a special season presented for two weeks at the Palais des Sports in Paris (and repeated, with a different supporting cast, for a Broadway season the following winter). This comprised *Apollo,* the *Flower Festival* pas de deux, *Aureole* and *The Moor's Pavane.* For an audience, it offered a rewarding mixture of styles: classic and modern, pure dance and drama, joyous and tragic. From a practical point of view, at a time of economic difficulties, it had the immense advantage that all the ballets require only a small cast— *Apollo,* with seven dancers, is the biggest. Since Nureyev and Merle Park danced in every ballet, and the French ballerina Wilfride Piollet in everything except the pas de deux, the whole program could be danced by a company of only nine (all of them, except Park and Nureyev, drawn from the Paris Opéra). Yet the effect was not one of a small-scaled show, thanks to the way the choreography used the full extent of the big stage.

As a demonstration of virtuosity, this was impressive, but there were some drawbacks. Perhaps because he wanted to make a more vivid contrast with the other works, Nureyev danced *Flower Festival* with an exuberance which

was exhilarating but perhaps too flamboyant for Bournonville's crisp, simple style. To the other three ballets he
brought his usual strong grasp of the right manner, coupled
with fine dancing, so it is carping to say that, watching the
program on two successive nights, there were moments
when it seemed he might have done marginally better in
one or another role if he had not tried to achieve so much in
the course of one evening and to sustain that effort for a
continuous run of performances. That is a counsel of perfection, because no dancer can really be expected to maintain his absolute peak all the time, but it is possible to see
dangers if he tried to sustain a program of that sort for more
than a limited run. Also, the likelihood of finding one partner able to dance all the different female roles equally well
is remote: Park and Piollet are both good dancers, but neither could match his range. However, as a manifesto of one
of the guiding principles of his career, the attempt to interpret in an authentic but personal way many different
moods, styles and periods, the occasion was stimulating
and successful. Also, as so often in the past, he brought to
prominence a promising young talent, that of Charles Jude,
picked from the Opéra's junior ranks to dance the other
male role in *Aureole*.

At the beginning of the new season, Nureyev was back in
Paris for two further new productions. The first was his
own revival of the Kingdom of Shades from *La Bayadère*.
Although his production for the Royal Ballet had remained
in the repertory, he had never mounted this work anywhere
else, and there would be few companies with a corps de ballet capable of meeting its technical and stylistic demands.
A really unified ensemble had not, in recent years, been
among the virtues of the Ballet de l'Opéra, but a new director, Raymond Franchetti, had been trying to change this.

They did at first have difficulty with *Bayadère,* especially the long opening dance with its many sustained arabesques, but by the time I saw it, at the seventh performance, they appeared not only to be coming to grips with the technique, but to be feeling the lilt of the mainly waltz rhythms of Minkus' music.

The *Bayadère* revival opened the 1974–75 season. Six weeks later, on November 13, Nureyev took the title role in the creation of *Tristan,* commissioned by the Opéra from Glen Tetley to a new score by Henze. The music, for solo piano, a large orchestra and electronic tape, lasted almost three-quarters of an hour and included allusions to Wagner and other composers, a short narrative read by a child's voice and episodes inspired by a nightmare, by the death of one of the composer's close friends and by the events in Chile beginning with the assassination of Salvador Allende. The vast scope of the piece, its formal and emotional contrasts, made it difficult to take in the shape and quality of the music at first hearing in a concert hall; dozens of people had walked out of the premiere at the Royal Festival Hall the previous month, and many London music critics were baffled by the work. When given as a ballet, the music became more readily accessible because events onstage helped define its structure.

It was the composer who suggested that his music should be used as a ballet for Nureyev, who, he said, since *Tancredi* "has asked me for many years to do some more music for him." Henze also nominated Tetley (who had already made a ballet, *Gemini,* to the composer's third symphony) as choreographer. In a program note, Tetley wrote how his choreography had been inspired by the subject and by his cast, in which Carolyn Carlson played Isolde: "When he came to the west, after his training at the Kirov, Nureyev became an enthusiast for everything that was new. He went everywhere. He began to study the different approaches of the classical technique and the modern technique. He has often come to see me, since the first years after his departure from the Soviet Union. . . . Nureyev has a fantastic appetite, he wants to know everything, he has the capacity constantly to change and extend his technique.

"Carolyn Carlson comes from another world, that of the modern dance. I was very excited by the idea of bringing together these two different personalities because I knew that each would find the possibility of enriching their technique. While working on *Tristan,* we created movements from improvisations, but not in any systematic way. Carolyn already knew this way of working. Rudolf took to it without the slightest problem.

"Ever since I have thought about Tristan and Isolde, I saw Nureyev's musculature and Carlson's silhouette. I thought of the Celtic origins of the legend with their distinctly physical character. The idealisation of the myth came later. Wagner introduced a psychoanalytical dimension into it and charged it with symbols. The Celtic version is sensual. Humour and adventure are present. . . . I saw this marvellous archaic figure of Isolde in Carolyn Carlson, in the emphasised length. And in my mind Nureyev's musculature represented this attraction, this force which pushed them together. I like differences, oppositions. There is a magical opposition between Carolyn Carlson and Rudolf Nureyev, exactly the one which could have existed between Tristan and Isolde."

The absence of any plot or chonological development in the ballet (Tetley likened it to a tapestry) made the roles difficult to sustain at such length. Isolde was already onstage when the curtain rose, Tristan soon joined her, and thereafter neither of them went off. Also, Tetley had again given the most spectacular moments to the subsidiary characters. Nureyev's part was based to a great extent on balances, extensions, slow falls and turns. It demanded immense strength and control, and to remain the center of attention in his quiet way would have been impossible without the powerful presence he possesses. I doubt whether any other dancer could have carried the work as he did (it would certainly have been a very different ballet without him). And once again it did represent an extension of his way of working, his grasp of different kinds of movement and ways of using movement. But it was a logical and predictable extension, not the revelation of something unexpected and surprising.

Nureyev once told me that he had one unfulfilled ambition: "Nobody has yet given me a part which surprised me and told me something about myself which I did not know already. My ambition is to be *discovered* by choreographers. I believe there is something in me that is still waiting to be found." He has had several new roles since then, and when talking about the ballets he dances or the choreographers he works with, he is always quick to point out their individual merits, often in a revealing way, with insight. But I suspect it will have to be a very astute, strong and cunning man who digs deeper into Nureyev than he has done himself.

He goes on searching for whatever in him is still undiscovered. Even before *Tristan,* he had been to work at the Martha Graham School in New York in preparation for proposed guest appearances with the Graham company, starting with a fund-raising gala in June, 1975. One of the great founding figures of modern dance, with a style that is starker than most of her successors, more sharply differentiated from classical ballet, Martha Graham created a new work, *Lucifer,* for Nureyev. At the gala premiere, when Fonteyn also appeared, ticket prices ranged up to $10,000. While this book goes through the press, Rudi van Dantzig and the American modern dancer Murray Louis are preparing to create new ballets with Nureyev, who is also announced for new roles in works by Béjart and the Danish choreographer Flemming Flindt on a tour with the Scottish Ballet.

In the classics, too, Nureyev has not been marking time. During a London season by the National Ballet of Canada, he played for the first time the part of Franz in *Coppelia,* keeping the characterization very light and humorous. The production was by Erik Bruhn, who himself played Dr. Coppelius; surprisingly, it was the first time the two friends had appeared together on a London stage. Nureyev learned and danced the role between rehearsals for a new production of *The Sleeping Beauty* which he was mounting for London Festival Ballet. He danced the first run of performances with Eva Evdokimova, one of the company's own principals, then partnered the former Kirov dancer Galina Panova (wife of Valery Panov, about whose difficulties in leaving the Soviet Union there had been such an outcry) in her London debut. Nureyev's agreeing to work in London with this rival company led to a certain coolness for a time on the part of the Royal Ballet, although they had shown no interest in having that production themselves and had not invited him to appear with them at that particular time. As Nureyev mildly remarked, "I have to make work for myself." Immediately after the *Beauty,* he began work on another revival, this time of his *Raymonda* for American Ballet Theatre.

With someone who works at such speed and intensity, any account must be unfinished. By the time his last activity has been recorded he is already on to something else. And the frustrating thing is that in a way, what comes next is more interesting than what has happened so far. While he continues dancing, it is certain that he will go on making new opportunities for himself, finding new ways to stretch his talents even further.

That is what keeps him ahead of the field. That, and the intensity of every performance. Remarking once that "it's quite difficult to dance, you know," he went on to elaborate that in a vivid metaphor: "It needs commitment and passion; every time you dance it must be sprayed with your blood. So much effort for so little reward—not from the public and critics, I mean, or the box office, but from yourself." The standard of perfection he sets for himself was revealed by something Erik Bruhn told me after one particular performance of *Don Quixote* at which Nureyev had danced notably well: "But he was upset because he missed a pirouette, and because of that, he could not sleep all night. I get like that, too; however well things go, if you do one thing badly, it spoils the evening, although of course you do not let it show, or let the audience realize you are unhappy; you smile nicely and thank them for the applause."

That is one of the reasons why Nureyev is, as he admits, "greedy for performances." Conscious of how short a dancer's career can be, he wants to cram in as much as possible. And he argues that since any dancer gives some performances when he is really on form, others when he cannot help being less than his best, "the more you do altogether, the more good ones there will be among them."

For the time being, he is first and foremost a dancer; his other activities take second place to that, and when he has the chance to do something else, even, for instance, the

122

Don Quixote film, he weighs its advantages against the amount of time it will take from his dancing career. By combining his innate talent with single-mindedness, persistence, determination and a kind of genius, Nureyev has made himself both a great dancer and a star. But he is more than just a dancer, more than just a star, and he is going to continue growing as an artist.

One obvious sphere for this is the extension of his choreographic activities. He is modest about these: "I am not yet sure if I am a choreographer. It takes total involvement, more than I can have while I am still dancing. And it's very difficult to choreograph a ballet for yourself to dance, because you go into your antics and there is nobody to tell you to stop."

Even so, he is all the time preparing himself. He is always thinking about steps in their context. Telling me once about a dance Leonid Yakobson had created for him and Sizova, he commented that one step was very like a passage in Balanchine's *Serenade,* then added reflectively that actually it is also done by the two gypsy women in *Petrushka,* where it looks completely different. Another example: Fanny Elssler came into the conversation once, and he remarked that she "must have been very beautiful. That Cachucha is short and very simple, and to succeed in it, she must have had the audience eating out of her hand as soon as she came onstage. Still, it was very interesting to see. I learned one step from it which I didn't know, and I used it in *Don Quixote.*"

The wish to turn more actively to choreography one day is one reason for his wanting to dance as many roles as possible, especially in new works. "You learn so much more about the structure of a ballet when you are actually in the

123

middle of it, much more than by watching." An advantage of mounting his new versions of the classics is that through these "I teach myself stagecraft."

There are, incidentally, still one or two other classics which he would like to revive. "I try to convince Michael Wood that one day I should mount the whole of *La Bayadère* for the Royal Ballet School. I think it should be done before it is all forgotten, and it would be more practicable to do it with students than professionally. It would be good for them to be in a full production. I think they should send someone to Russia to photograph the original sets, which are all painted. They would not be expensive to reproduce. Then I think *Pharaoh's Daughter* must have been one of Petipa's best ballets. There was a tradition at the Kirov that the music was very attractive, and the ballet was a long time in the repertory. I would like to find out more about it and if the notation of the choreography exists still."

Apart from choreography and production, there are at least two other possibilities open to him in the long term: to develop the start he has already made in films or, perhaps most rewardingly of all, to direct a ballet company. Suppose he had the chance of that, I asked him; would he be prepared to stop dancing in order to accept? "Not yet. I think I have another five years before I have to give up the classics or rather before they give me up; maybe seven years if I am lucky. I must do them while I can. And it would be difficult to direct a company and share out the roles fairly with the other dancers."

However, it is clear that his acquired expertise and his analytical mind give him the aptitude for directing a company. Talking about other dancers, for instance, he is always quick to point out what the logical next step in their careers should be, which are ready to be given more roles, which would be wise to look elsewhere for opportunities. He concerns himself, too, with all sorts of details that do not usually bother a dancer. As an example, he once remarked that he would really like to be given a list of past programs at Covent Garden because "I saw many of these and can remember which worked as a program and which did not. It would be interesting to try to analyze what makes good program building."

Whatever he turns to, I doubt that Nureyev will ever willingly divorce himself from appearing onstage. I asked him whether, when he eventually has to stop dancing the big classical leads, he would be prepared to continue with smaller or less demanding parts. "What choice do I have?" he asked. "And there are many small parts which it could be very interesting to do. I think that when a dancer's career begins, there is a bonus in the freshness of youth. Then comes a period when there is complete command. But after that, I don't think it is fair that a dancer should just be pushed aside when he still has something to offer. When someone has devoted his life to the stage, I think that as an artist he should be given the right to die onstage, too."

Close-Ups

NUREYEV offstage is a very private person. He mixes easily with people of all kinds but often seems a little wary, rather on his guard. The comparison that springs to mind is with a cat: walking confidently but delicately, responsive but reserved, ready to draw back from possessiveness or too much familiarity. There has to be a streak of ruthlessness in him; without it he could never have achieved what he has. But the turbulent side of his nature is usually well under control, and it is mixed anyway with a quiet, gentle quality and a mischievous sense of humor. He has dignity but does not stand on it; he is proud, but there is no *side* about him. It is not easy to know him well, but his friends adore him and are touched by his kindness and generosity, and I think it is difficult to know him at all without liking him.

In spite of his powerful muscles, the immediate physical impression he projects is of neatness. You notice the trim waist before the broad shoulders. When he dresses up, his clothes are elegant, often in a theatrical way. He smiles easily, his upper lip crinkling with amusement. His eyes are alert and inquiring; they miss nothing, yet when talking to someone he gives the impression of undivided attention.

His voice is quiet, attractively inflected, with a slight accent.

He relies on a few friends to help organize his everyday life and crowds in as much as he does by a process of elimination and concentration. He is adroit at avoiding activities which have no interest for him but is immensely thorough about everything he does undertake. In spite of the number of performances he gives and the traveling from one place to another to fit them all in, he is never too busy to help other dancers who ask for guidance about their roles.

He has the enviable ability to take a nap in the afternoon when his schedule allows that luxury; just as well, since he cannot usually lie abed in the mornings because of the timing of classes and rehearsals, and at night after performance he has to unwind slowly before he can sleep. That is generally accomplished over a meal with friends. His travels have helped him acquire a circle of friends in many cities, who are often drawn from outside the world of ballet. A welcome guest, he is also a thoughtful host, whether with one or two people for supper or a whole houseful at a party, each one of whom he tries to look after.

He makes time to go a lot to movies and the theater, and if he unavoidably misses a notable film or play, he questions other people closely about it. He is keenly interested in music and knowledgeable about painting. Manifestly well read, he speaks several languages with fair fluency, although he decries his skill as a linguist. He is always keen to learn the exact nuances of a word or phrase new to him; he wants it defined, then will probably ask just how it differs from another with similar meaning. When reading, he has a sharp eye for the implications that lie between the lines.

He plans his own career carefully, dovetailing one prospective engagement with another. Although he has agents to undertake the work of arranging contracts, he himself decides what engagements he will accept, laying his plans well ahead and himself taking the initiative if there is something that specially interests him.

His memory must be unusually good because he can specify the date of a future engagement without looking it up, and while I have been writing this book, he has managed to recall the details of events which happened twelve or fifteen years earlier. He has a sense of timing that gets him to the right place at the right time for any important engagement, although he never wears a watch. He has a reputation for being late which, in my experience, applies only to occasions when punctuality is no longer vital and he allows himself to be held up by something more pressing.

The first time I had any close dealings with him was in connection with an interview for the *Times*. We had already met, thanks to mutual friends, but knew each other only slightly. Most newspaper references to him were still somewhat sensational, and I thought perhaps the time was ripe to try to show a different side of him, the serious, hardworking, intelligent artist.

When I mentioned this idea to the Covent Garden press office, they were not very hopeful. Nureyev was reluctant to give interviews, they said, because he had so often been misrepresented, but if I liked to try my luck, I could get in touch with him myself at the Royal Ballet School. I left a note explaining what I wanted and giving my telephone number. In spite of gloomy forecasts, there was no problem; he telephoned himself (he has no secretary), agreed at once and fixed a date. Incidentally, when a change in his working commitments made it necessary for him to change the time slightly, he not only made sure that I got as much warning as possible, but took the trouble to call himself, confirming the message already sent.

That interview occupied a substantial part of two evenings. On the first, I think we were both nervous, but once we had got going I found that we talked at greater length than I had dared to hope, not only about the topics I had planned, but many others too. From that I wrote up an account of the most interesting parts and, following my regular practice, let him see a copy of the typescript for any corrections or second thoughts before it was printed. This proved to be far from the formality it usually is. He wanted to meet again and go in detail through the draft.

What impressed me was the insight he showed into the possible implications of every word. "Yes, I said all that, but some of it perhaps I should not have said" was his first reaction, which made my spirits sink. However, when he produced his copy of the draft, it was covered with annotations in the margin and between the lines, and I finished with more additions than cuts. I never knew anyone ask for so many changes, but the result was well worthwhile.

For every change he wanted, he had a reason. One reference to another dancer might be hurtful, he thought, and although the dancer in question had shown a lack of insight in the episode Nureyev had described to me, that was explained by his background; he could not have been expected to do anything else. Could we perhaps leave out his name and any identifying description? There were some interesting comments he had made on the individual qualities of certain choreographers, all of them favorable, picking out the aspects in which each was strongest. Those he wanted deleted because they were only his opinions, and he did not like the idea of any creative artist's being tagged in this way.

Several passages, on the other hand, he wanted to elaborate so that they expressed his ideas more exactly. The final result was a much more interesting interview than would have been the case if he had not helped revise it. This was my first glimpse of the way his own intense professionalism extends to an insight into the professional problems and needs of other trades.

There was further opportunity to observe this when I became marginally involved in the making of the film *I Am a Dancer,* during which it was easy to see how well he gets on with other people who are good at their own jobs, but bunglers of any sort annoy him.

My association with the film began with a telephone call from its producer, John Hargreaves. He did not exactly start off "You may have heard of a dancer called Rudolf Nureyev . . ." but the conversation was veering that way. Later, I realized that the reason for his careful explanation of every point, including several that I knew perfectly well already, must have been a conviction, acquired through experience, that in the film world you can never take anything for granted. Certainly the way that film progressed, by a series of crises and reversals, toward its deadline for completion proved hectically dramatic.

My share on the sidelines involved rewriting the commentary. The original French television production, made the previous year, had a commentary by the French writer Jean Cau which Nureyev, when he belatedly heard it, found embarrassingly fulsome. He wanted something cooler, more detached, and thought I might be a suitable person to do it. The assignment was flattering and interesting, but not altogether satisfying. One problem was that the film had already been edited to fit the original French text, so my first instructions were to produce a new commentary that would occupy as closely as possible the same amount of time. Some extra sequences were to be added, but the idea was that slipping them into the film would not greatly affect the balance and they would need only a few words of introduction.

Later, after some meetings I attended and others I only heard about, the running order was much changed, and the very long classroom scenes of the original version were truncated. That was a pity, because for me the sight of Nureyev in exercises at the barre, in center practice and trying various solos was one of the most fascinating things in the film. Many people thought the same even about the shorter classroom sequences which remained in the final version. Unfortunately, he had been filmed wearing different garments, an error hidden originally by breaking up the sequence with interpolations of irrelevant scenes: Nureyev resting, for instance, or joking with a big towel around his head like a turban. These shots looked silly in their context, and it was decided that they had to be removed. The moment that had been done the other problem became obvious. One of the passages that had to be deleted in consequence was especially interesting: a slow-motion version of Nureyev, in practice clothes, going through one of his solos from *La Sylphide*. Even without the proper music (which would have sounded absurd, played so slowly, so someone had dubbed in some electronic tinkling sounds), the meticulous detail of his technique, the muscular perfection with which he executed the steps, were brilliantly revealed.

It soon became clear to everyone that there was a lack of rapport between Nureyev and one of the film men involved with the additional sequences. The filmmaker has a distinguished reputation in his own field but possibly fancied his expertise in ballet a little more than was justified. He was also inclined to act the star during the filming sessions, which would obviously clash with Nureyev's undemonstrative concentration on the work in hand. Besides, there was no time for chichi because everything else had to be fitted in with Nureyev's busy schedule of performances.

The extracts from *Field Figures* were put into the film at Nureyev's insistence. The only other modern work included was *Marguerite and Armand,* and even this follows a fairly conventional narrative line. On his usual principle of wanting to show as wide a range as possible, Nureyev picked this very new work which he was then preparing to dance for the first time onstage. Most of the film people were apprehensive about public reaction to such an uncompromising modern work with its "difficult" Stockhausen score, lack of story line and unusual style of movement. In the event, the contrast with the more traditional ballets in the film proved stimulating and refreshing, and the fidelity of the picture as a portrait of its subject was much enhanced.

This sequence was shot one bitterly cold evening in the Donmar studios, just off Charing Cross Road. To admit cables for the powerful film lights, big doors at one end had to be left ajar and a cutting draft blew in, which even for warmly dressed bystanders was decidedly uncomfortable. At one point Nureyev asked whether the air conditioning could not be switched off, and the source of the cold air had to be broken to him. For dancers in light costumes, needing warm muscles, this was not very helpful.

There came a moment when Nureyev and Deanne Bergsma were having trouble getting to grips with some tricky partnering. They broke off to confer with Tetley, who was in London to work with Nureyev on the role. Before resuming, Nureyev decided that his hair needed combing. Dissatisfied with the result, he did it a second time. Then came a further pause to look for the spray to hold it in position during the involved and energetic movement. Cameramen and technicians grew restless during this pause, but Nureyev neatly punctured the tension and got everyone back in the right mood by turning to them as soon as he was ready, giving a broad grin and purring the one word "Pretty?"

It was again bleak weather when the pas de deux, solos and coda from the last act of *The Sleeping Beauty* were filmed on Sunday at the Coliseum. Nureyev was suffering from a cold. He was also unhappy because the director had set up two of the three cameras right around the sides of the dress circle. This position, he was convinced, would prove largely useless. The outcome proved him right. From this angle the dance was seen out of its intended perspective, and an added disadvantage was that the dancers were seen against the blackness of the wings instead of the scenery which had been hired (from Festival Ballet's production) for the filming.

This vindication cannot have proved much comfort. But in spite of all vexations, Nureyev went patiently on, dancing his solo over and over again because it was not satisfying him. The ideal arrangement would have been to try again another day, but that was just not practicable, so he continued until at last each section had come right. All this was done to a solo piano accompaniment and the orchestra dubbed in later, as was the applause heard in the film. He and Lynn Seymour were actually filmed taking their bows to the modest applause of the small audience who for one reason or another had come along to watch the filming.

When it came to editing the film, Nureyev proved well informed about the techniques involved and aware of what would produce the best result. In late-night sessions at a small preview theater I saw him going through passages with the editor, Timothy Gee, suggesting in minute detail what could be done to improve the rough version. I imagine it must have been this experience which convinced Nureyev, when it came to filming *Don Quixote* a year later, that he would be best advised to direct it himself.

Meanwhile, my own contribution to the film was having to be changed to fit the revised running order and contents. In retrospect, it is easy to see that the best course would have been to scrap the first version entirely and start from scratch, but that became clear only when it was too late. Even so, two drastic revisions followed each other quickly. John Hargreaves wanted to persuade Nureyev to speak the commentary himself, so I was asked to adapt it into the first person. Not liking to put words in someone else's mouth—especially somebody so clear-sighted about what he does—I tried as far as possible to make up the text from his own remarks, either during the filming or in various past interviews. The comments on *Field Figures* were taken from a letter Tetley had written about how he created it.

But Nureyev was reluctant to speak the commentary himself. The deadline for recording it was fast approaching, and he was now in Zurich producing and dancing *Raymonda*. I was dispatched there to agree on a final version with him, but he was clearly unhappy about the whole business and, although perfectly charming, put off discussing it as long as possible. We drank tea in his hotel; a group of us went off to see a terrible movie, traveling by tram (where nobody seemed to recognize him); afterward he took us all to supper in the best restaurant in town, where he *was* recognized and a table found with little delay although the place was full. Eventually we discussed the script over lunch the next day. He arrived late because he had somehow got locked out of his dressing room in the theater wearing only practice clothes, with all his street clothes shut inside. He was adamant about not speaking the script himself (partly, I suspect, because of his reservations about the film as a whole) but full of helpful suggestions about how to adapt it into a new version for someone else to read.

It was in August, 1973, on a tour to Israel by the Royal Ballet's smaller company, that I had the opportunity to watch Nureyev working, offstage as well as on, for most of the day over a period of more than a week. My wife and I were offered the chance to travel with the company for the whole trip. We and the company left London on a Thursday morning; Nureyev had to follow behind, two days later, because he was dancing at Covent Garden on Friday night. All this was when he had just returned from dancing the series of performances of *Swan Lake* in Paris during which Makarova went off in a huff. On getting back to London, he had only two days in which to work with the company on the repertory they would be dancing together. After that he had to rehearse with Merle Park for the *Swan Lake* they were giving at Covent Garden on Wednesday (a different version from the one he had been doing with other partners in Paris), and with Lynn Seymour for *Romeo and Juliet,* which they danced together the night before flying to Tel Aviv.

In Israel, rehearsals were going ahead. The repertory was being fitted onto the stage of the Mann Auditorium, where two of the performances were to be given. All the ballets had to be tried out with the local orchestra, too, and the

136

Haifa Symphony was proving woefully inadequate, all the more so because it had to be supplemented for the occasion and the extra players, drawn from army bands, were not available for some rehearsals. Also, *Prodigal Son* and *The Corsair* pas de deux were both new to this company's repertory, and *Apollo* had a new cast of muses, so these needed to be worked on.

Peter Clegg, the ballet master, explained on Saturday how he was getting ready for Nureyev's arrival: "He's due at seven thirty this evening, but remember how our plane was held up. I don't suppose he'll be at the hotel before nine at the earliest. I must talk to him then about what he wants to do tomorrow. It's very difficult to decide; I've tried to prepare everything, leaving the options open. He has to dance four ballets tomorrow and rehearse. The theater where we are giving the early performance is said to have a good stage, but the later one is poor. We've got linoleum, but Rudolf might not like to use that. It can be dangerously slippery, and he has some tricky things to do."

Clegg's estimate of arrival time was about right. Nureyev had come offstage about ten thirty the previous night after dancing three strenuous acts of *Romeo and Juliet*. After that he had to eat and allow himself time to unwind from the tension of performing before he could sleep. Not surprisingly, he got to Heathrow at the very last minute and, because of the strict security checks on flights to Tel Aviv, had to take his case himself to the tarmac for clearance. There, he told us, his strange collection of garments caused some astonishment. As well as clothes for wearing in Israel, then on vacation and after that in Milan, he had with him costumes for the Israel performances, old tights and shoes for class, and a further set of costumes for his performances at La Scala immediately after his holiday. With so much to remember, some things got forgotten, and on arrival he had to borrow a razor and swimming trunks.

Nureyev hates flying but forces himself to do it all the time because it is the only way he can manage all the performances he wants to undertake. The five-hour journey to Tel Aviv must have been as trying to his nerves as to his muscles, cramped in a sitting position, but within a short time of landing he looked remarkably cheerful. It was about half past midnight when we ran into him; we had just come back from a gossipy supper in a Jaffa restaurant when he came in through the doors of the Hilton. Wearing a droopy white sweater and a big knitted black cap, he came up, grinning happily, to say good-night to us and a couple of dancers. "Why a woolly hat in this heat?" somebody asked, and he replied, "For the air conditioning inside the buildings."

The next morning saw a startling transformation. There were to be two performances that day, in two different theaters in Jerusalem. Most of the dancers were to travel by coach, but a few principals had to go ahead by car. Soon after eleven forty-five everyone was waiting in the lobby when the taxis arrived. Someone rang upstairs to tell Nureyev they were ready. There followed an expectant pause, during which hovering press photographers edged closer to the elevators. Around the corner came the star, dressed in a tight white satin suit with white shoes, and the woolly hat now looking far more glamorous in its new context, but carrying his own bags with shoes and other essentials. On seeing the photographers, he at once dropped the bags on the floor and obligingly strolled about, smiling for the cameras. But although willing to go through the ritual expected of a star, he was quick to go up to Seymour at the earliest opportunity, embracing her and making sure she got in the pictures, too.

That was to be a long day. The main body of dancers, their coach held up by a truck drivers' slowdown, reached the Jerusalem Theater a little before two thirty. All afternoon there were rehearsals, preceded only by a warm-up class. The first house, a charity show in aid of handicapped children, was due to start at six thirty but was unavoidably delayed. Nureyev had not originally been announced for this program, but there were so many requests for him to appear that he eventually agreed to dance *Apollo*, which was put first on the bill so as to give him a short break before the later show. That was to be given in the Binyenei Ha'oomah, a huge new concert hall a little way from the Jerusalem Theater. The stage there was large but with a poor surface, and because the audience was already being seated by the time the dancers were able to arrive, there was no chance for them to try the stage before the first ballet.

This was *Les Rendezvous*, again with Nureyev. Later in that program he had another role in the virtuoso *Corsair* pas de deux, followed after an interval by a further performance of *Apollo*. When the final work ended, Nureyev might have been expected to be rather tired, but by the time the rest of us reached the Jerusalem Tower Hotel, where the British ambassador was giving the whole party supper, he was already there. The journey back to Tel Aviv did not start until nearly three in the morning, but Nureyev was still looking cheerfully wide awake, clowning around as he waved off the coachload of sleepy dancers before getting into his taxi.

His first public appearance the next day, however, was not until nearly four in the afternoon. This was a rest day, and a party had gone off sightseeing, but some of us stayed behind at the swimming pool. Nureyev joined us while we were sitting at the terrace snack bar and said, "I just slept." Later it turned out that his sleep had been interrupted, from eight o'clock onward, by a number of telephone calls, including one from a Jewish friend in New York to wish him *shalom*.

By now people knew that he was around, and all the time his presence attracted a lot of attention. While he was eating a hamburger, he was interrupted first by a lady, a complete stranger, who wanted him to get her tickets for the sold-out performances, then by a man wanting autographs ("Two, please, on separate sheets"). He got what he wanted, the lady did not, but both were dealt with quietly and charmingly, although Nureyev could reasonably have hoped to be allowed his meal in peace.

The next day there was class and rehearsal at the Mann Auditorium and a performance there in the evening. Nureyev was one of the first to arrive. Asked, "How are you?" he replied laconically, "Present." "Here physically and spiritually" came the comment, which he amended to "Well, here bodily." Drinking one of his endless cups of sweet tea in the canteen before class began, he leaned on the counter and painfully stretched his leg, commenting, "when I was young, I had such loose legs: extensions front, back, sides, right up to here"—indicating his shoulder level—"but then it all went into jump. Now it takes me all day to be able to stretch them."

In class he takes some exercises at a different speed from the other dancers, to suit his own muscles and the needs of the roles he is going to perform. A set of grands battements, for instance, he does at half the speed set, so that he is still with the music but making a more powerful movement of the leg as it swings. One set of jumps he misses, because he is busy pulling on a third pair of tights to keep the muscles warm, but Seymour wants to try them again more slowly, and he joins in, interpolating pauses during which he holds his position absolutely steady. At times he appears to be paying no attention while an exercise is set (once he is busy practicing ronds de jambe, for instance, and another time stretching and pressing against the wall), but it is clear all the same that he has grasped it. At a class in different circumstances Nureyev will do what the teacher sets and accept correction, but here the only concern is to be ready for the night's performance. This individual approach is obviously not a matter of showing off but simply of getting the best value from the time available. He is observant and considerate all the time, too; when Seymour comments that the floor is slippery, he goes off and finds the last remaining rosin to sprinkle around.

While the linoleum floor is being laid for the *Prodigal Son* rehearsal, he is busy practicing his pirouettes for that night's *Corsair* and his entrechats for *Apollo*. When Clegg consults him about the right initial position for the piece of scenery that serves variously as a table and (upside down) as garden gates and the sides of a boat, Nureyev is pragmatic about it. "Well, put it here, and we'll find out."

When he comes to his exit at the end of the first scene, it is obvious that the wings are placed so far back that he cannot carry out the normal sequence of leaping forward over the gate, spinning in a pirouette, making a gesture of shouting back to his abandoned family and then falling backwards out of sight. He comes down into the auditorium and looks at the table from both sides and the center, working out what adjustment is necessary. While he is doing this, the line of bizarre drinking companions make their en-

141

trance, swinging in a smart detour around the fence, which they then lift and upend to turn it into a table. At once Nureyev is there, showing the exact spot where it needs to be put down and suggesting that it would be a good idea to have marks on the floor to guide them.

Making his next entry, he does a comic version of his mime instead of playing it straight. I notice other dancers doing something similar at rehearsals during the week. It must be difficult to go solemnly through acting a role when you are constantly being interrupted for one reason or another, when you are having to concern yourself also with what everyone else is and ought to be doing and when you are not wearing makeup or costume either. Nureyev's practice clothes are chosen for comfort, not appearance. As usual, he is wearing several layers, and his pale-blue woolen tights have stretched and hang baggily, drooping around his loins, sagging at the crotch, thighs and knees.

At the end of the scene where he is beaten up before being robbed, he calls out, "The light change was too soon." Probably misunderstanding his point and thinking he was concerned only to be seen clearly, the stage director replies, "There'll be a spot on you tomorrow night, but at the moment it's fixed for *Apollo.*" Nureyev soon puts him right on this: "But the light shouldn't change at all during that number; it was two bars too soon."

For the Prodigal's last entrance, Nureyev sees that there will be difficulty because of the placing of the gate in relation to the wings. He suggests to the stage staff, "I think I had better come on before you put any light on." Ashley Lawrence, the conductor, comments, "I'll wait until I see you before I start the music," and Nureyev replies, "But I'll be coming in the dark." However, they decide it will be practicable. Later, when Nureyev is making his way across the stage, he interrupts himself and the orchestra: "Sorry, could you stop please? I think we should get this sorted out. Do you think you could put some light on this scene—two lamps at the side here? It's all far too dark." When this is done, it proves right.

That night, after the performance (a repeat of the main Jerusalem program), Nureyev takes some of the leading dancers and staff out to supper. In spite of this and a late-night dip in the sea on returning to the hotel, he has enough energy the next morning to persuade two of the other dancers to teach him the theory of how to sail a boat, then to take him out for his first attempt.

There is another rehearsal of *Prodigal* in the afternoon. At the point where the Prodigal is thrown against a pillar by his assailants, Ashley Lawrence asks, "Rudi, is it possible for you to be there any sooner?" "Yes." "Because it's difficult to hold that note." "No problem."

When Seymour, who is dancing the siren for the first time, has some trouble (like most people in this role) manipulating her long, heavy cloak, Nureyev is able to advise her how to manage it. Later he demonstrates, perched across one corner of the table, just how she should sit on his shoulders for one tricky lift. During the rehearsal, too, he is getting the prodigal's two traveling companions into line by beckoning or pushing them as needed. After his own first exit he comes back during the final bars of the music to check the practicability of getting to the wings in spite of their awkward position.

In the intermission at that night's performance, he is limbering up in the tiny space available in the wings; impossible to go onstage for this, as there is no curtain. He greets a friend with the comment "You see how much space they give me. How can I practice jumps?" Somehow, he manages to jump impressively in spite of the difficulties. Life that week is a question of compromise. In the open-air theater at Caesarea the next night, for instance, there is just one big dressing room for the whole company, in a space under the stage—catacombs, one dancer calls it with justice. Nureyev's table is at one end, but to get to it from the stage, he has to climb over one safety rail, under another, then down a winding metal staircase. The alternative to climbing the rails is a long detour. In these circumstances, he and several other dancers have to manage a number of quick changes during the evening.

On the Friday night (the Sabbath, so no performance), the British ambassador gives a reception for the company in his garden. Nureyev arrives after spending the day visiting Jerusalem and Bethlehem in a hired car; he is disappointed in his driver-guide who only knows the standard comments off by heart and is unable to answer his fare's questions about exactly what happens everywhere and why. Mrs. Ledwige proves a tactful hostess; instead of treating Nureyev like an exhibit for her other guests, she places him at a table with several of his friends. After eating, Nureyev does his duty, saying to Seymour, "Well, I think we should plunge into the crowd." On the way back to the hotel afterward he is given a lift by one of the embassy families. He takes great trouble over autographs for their children. In return, he picks their brains about local conditions for his new enthusiasm, sailing.

There are two more performances to go, one of them a special gala at which crowds of celebrities are present. Rehearsals that day have been interrupted by special security arrangements because the Prime Minister is coming to see the company, and somehow the audience starts to throng into the huge stone amphitheater while Nureyev is still practicing his *Corsair* solo. They are so obsessed with finding their seats, and presumably have such preconceptions about how stars behave, that nobody seems to recognize the dancer hurtling around the stage without music and wearing layers of baggy old tights.

Somehow during these final days Nureyev finds time also to coach Nicholas Johnson and Brenda Last, at their request, in the *Flower Festival* duet and to pursue his sailing to the point that before leaving Tel Aviv, he passes a test of seamanship and gets the certificate needed before he is allowed to take a boat outside the harbor on his own. The morning after the last performance he is away early for the first real holiday he has had in quite a long time.

Having heard so much from dancers about Nureyev's way of preparing a production, I wanted to see for myself how he went about it and asked to be allowed to watch rehearsals of *The Nutcracker*. This was not a new production from scratch, but a revival for the Royal Ballet after a lapse of four years, during which time there had been many changes in the company. Consequently, many of the dancers were new to their roles. Also, Nureyev was taking the opportunity of introducing a great many changes into his choreography.

On my first day, rehearsal was due to begin soon after midday, immediately after company class. Arriving in the big studio where, according to the schedule, Nureyev was due to work with the corps de ballet on the Valse des Fleurs, I find him about to leave this under Michael Somes' supervision. He explains, "They are working on the Spanish dance in the other room. I think I must go and torture them." It soon becomes clear that it is one of the dances to be altered.

In the smaller studio we find half a dozen dancers, a pianist and Desmond Doyle, the ballet master. Work begins with the opening phrase of the dance, but Nureyev stops Michael Coleman, who is taking the male role. "You are doing your beats upright; I do mine at an angle," he says, and demonstrates. Coleman tries again, differently, and is stopped once more: "No, don't bend your body towards your feet."As he tries it a third time, Nureyev explains what he is after: "Try to finish the beats before you straighten up; it looks lighter and easier." Obviously it is not actually easier to do, but they go on working at it. Although very specific about the effect he wants, Nureyev gives no sign of regarding his choreography as sacrosanct. When Laura Connor asks which arm should be raised at the end of one phrase, he asks her which is the more comfortable—or "the least painful."

They come to a passage where the dancers perform a series of échappés traveling and turning across the stage to produce an effect like a typical Spanish step. Nicholas Johnson, also learning the role, does not at first get it quite as Nureyev wants. "A bigger movement," he is told, "cross your legs more—back to audience." Then Nureyev counts out the rhythm to him, with heavy emphasis and slightly unexpected timing; this does the trick by giving Johnson the phrasing he needs.

Going back to repeat the passage that led to this step, the dancers have trouble fitting in the links from a big lift. First Nureyev tries to get them to move quicker and prepare ahead ("You're not thinking where you are going to go"), but it still does not work smoothly, so he abandons the échappés altogether and devises a new set of movements for that music. In fact, he does two versions, both based on strong arm movements but starting with opposite arms up and progressing differently. Then he has the dancers perform both and picks the one he prefers. Because the dance is short, his aim seems to be to use a lot of fine detail. "It's a quart in a pint pot," Coleman comments, and has to explain the idiom, which happens to be new to Nureyev.

We hurry back to watch the end of the Valse des Fleurs in the other room. Next comes the Russian dance, another for which Nureyev is doing a new version. First he shows the dancers how they will make their entrance in a line sideways across the stage, turn and bow to the audience, then face each other and bow again. At this point they begin to collide with each other, the comic surprise effect he intended. "Can we do this?" they ask, rubbing imaginary bruises, and he replies, "Yes, just be natural." But timing is crucial: He wants the first bow slow, then quick confusion followed by a smart return to order. This has to be done before the music starts, so they try it once or twice and settle upon two counts of six to give them the timing.

Now Nureyev sets the opening phrase: the men bursting forward, the girls grabbing them by the wrist, pulling them back and themselves swaggering to the front, with the men following more sedately. When Nureyev starts to show the next step, strong and assertive, Betty Anderton asks, "Do the ladies do this, too?" Unexpectedly comes the answer, "It's for you."

The next phrase has some circling movements. "Don't go backwards," he calls to the girl on the outside of one line. "You must stay still, as pivot," and to emphasize the point, he pretends to hammer a nail into the top of her head to fix her to the spot. The lines are arranged with the pivot dancer upright, the others progressively more crouched; the inner

147

ones, with their knees most bent, are having trouble getting right around, and he shows the big, low steps they will need.

Now he is correcting them more often when anything goes wrong. "You must be quicker," he tells one group of girls after a passage where they make extravagant gestures poking fun at the men. "I think you must start straight away to run to the other side." When they are having trouble bourréeing round on their heels, supported by the men, he comments, "If you don't lean on him so much, it's easier." At one point Anderton has to fall forward and be caught from behind by David Drew, and they have trouble sorting out how best to manage it. Nureyev tries it himself and finds the knack: "Pull like this."

Later the dancers have to run in couples around the stage with long, loping strides, their arms stretched straight out sideways and swaying slightly as they go. Nureyev explains the effect as "flying," but Anderton comments realistically, after their slightly disastrous first attempt (at which she, but few others, got the point), "I don't think the English temperament understands flying." Again Nureyev shows what he wants, explaining, "Don't move your arms; if you go *right* and *left* with your hips"—pushing them forward emphatically on alternate steps to show what he means—"it all comes from there."

That is the end of *The Nutcracker* rehearsals for the day, because Nureyev has to make his debut that evening in *Agon*. Incidentally, his only refreshment all this while has been three plastic beakers of tea, brought to him all together, carried on the lid of a cardboard box.

The next day he is at it again early; class is at ten thirty, for which he needs to leave his Richmond home soon after nine thirty. I arrive at noon and find the cast of the Arabian dance assembling in the small studio. Nureyev is detained, running through *The Sleeping Beauty* pas de deux with Jennifer Penney, because they have arranged to dance it together in a couple of gala performances at Monte Carlo the following week. He sends a message for the dancers to watch a film of the dance so that they know what to expect.

Soon he arrives, with a very quiet "Good morning," and goes to look for a chair, which he sets down facing the dancers. They form themselves into the ring which begins the dance, sitting on the ground. They play a family eating from a big dish in the middle, bullied by an old man who will not let them help themselves but insists on distributing tidbits, with double helpings for his favorites and himself, none for those he disapproves. Leaving his chair and squatting on the floor with one leg tucked under him, Nureyev pulls faces to show the dancers what their reactions should be: smug delight for some, growing discontent for others. His exaggerated reactions provoke the dancers into grimaces which will carry across the footlights. They have to sort out the order of certain gestures, and although the others have just watched the film, it is Nureyev who is able to give them the details—not from any special trick of memory, it seems, but from the internal logic of the piece, both in the relationships of the characters and an awareness of who must move first to make someone else visible to the audience.

Vergie Derman and Julian Hosking leave the group for an exotic dance routine. When she hops up into his arms, Nureyev wants a bigger movement: "It should be a jump; she should fly through the air." He reminds Derman, "You must jump with your heels close together," because she has to land kneeling on the boy's flexed thigh. When Hosking tries to catch her rather high on his leg, Nureyev comments, "Unless you can pull her right up, it's more secure on the knee."

At one o'clock Merle Park and David Wall arrive to work on the new pas de deux that is going to start Act 2. They are to dance the leading parts together at some performances, although Park will do the first night with Nureyev. Penney, who will also dance *The Nutcracker* with Nureyev, and Lesley Collier, understudying the ballerina role, also turn up. During the subsequent activities they are repeating some of Park's movements, so far as is practicable without a partner, at the back of the room.

Park has her own views on how some of this should be done. Early in the session, when Nureyev suggests a different way of managing one lift, she answers, "If I could lift you, I'd show you." Obligingly, Nureyev straddles his legs across the barre fixed to the wall and supports himself there while they pursue the point. He is anxious that the movements in this duet should look right for a very young girl, this still being rather early in the dream sequences during which Clara grows up emotionally. When Park makes too seductive a gesture, he remarks, smiling, "I think she'll be raped by the time she's . . . what is it? Seven and a half?"

Someone comes from the other studio (where the corps de ballet are working on the Snowflakes scene) to call Nureyev to sort out a problem. While he is gone, Park and Wall try out alternative ways of tackling certain moments. On Nureyev's return, they tell him, "We found another way to do the underneath lift." When they show it, he comments, "Well, this is easiest. It shouldn't be exhausting because there is so much dancing ahead." On the same principle, when he notices they look tense about a movement, he says, "Any effort you have to make like that, you shouldn't do it." When they are working out how best to get Park back on the ground at one point, Wall carries her right across the room and sets her down gently, but Nureyev says, "I'm not concerned to carry her longer, I'm trying to get her off," at which they all laugh.

An experienced partner, Wall is contributing practical comments all this time: "She's on the wrong side; she's turning this way, and the angle of support is there." Nureyev considers his suggestions carefully, adapting the duet as necessary. They are taking trouble over details. "Don't forget you've a head in the way" is one comment. Park asks, "Did that look a bit rushed?" and Nureyev answers, "No it looks very calm." Collier, somewhat breathless at the back of the room, bursts into laughter at this and pulls a rueful face as he turns to her and asks, "No?"

There is a passage when Park has to lift her leg in an arc while lying across Wall's shoulder. "How big do you want me to do that?" she asks. "The more, the better." "When do you want me to start it?" His eyes glaze slightly as he starts to sing the music, apparently visualizing the movement. "Now?" Park asks at what seems the obvious moment, but he says, "Not yet," and goes on singing, making a big arm movement a few moments later to show both the start and the speed of the movement so that it is completed at the right point in the music. The dancers repeat the lift. "Not quite at the right angle, is it?" Park asks, but Nureyev answers, "Don't worry about the angle, I'm trying to see the right moment."

Again they are interrupted. A secretary brings some papers he needs; a dancer from another rehearsal comes to check a step in one of his other productions. The dancers are cheerfully responsive. Park, held upside down by Wall in one precarious lift and beginning to slip, jokes: "Go on— jeté!" Pleased with one effect, she says, "That's much more

little-girlish—ooh! Then I come right down on your leg."
Time passes quickly until at two forty-five Wall apologizes
that he has to leave for another rehearsal. Nureyev has left
himself only a quarter of an hour for lunch in the canteen
(cottage cheese, two boiled eggs, a dish of prunes, three cups
of sweet tea) before going up to join the Valse d'Or rehearsal
for the corps de ballet with the comment that he wants to
"clean it up a bit at the end."

They are working on a sequence where four couples
dance at the front. He lets them try it, then shows with a
kind of "shorthand" marking (the movements simplified
but the essential beat heavily stressed) how he wants it
done. Laura Connor and Gary Sinclaire, who danced one of
the couples in the previous production, demonstrate the
way they remember it. Nureyev goes through it himself,
first with Connor, then with Christine Aitken from the
new cast. The dancers try again; Nureyev watches pensive-
ly, biting the end of one finger, head tilted to one side.

He stops one of the girls and asks, "Can't you do that?"
Taking her partner's place, he does it with her, whereupon
she gets it right. "Let's see if you can do it in one line," he
says, and they try, but his comment is: "Yes, but that's supposed to be *in one line.*" He makes them do it again, this
time stamping out the rhythm so that nobody can miss it.
They go through the short phrase again and again, sometimes in small groups, sometimes all together. Somes, the
senior répétiteur, explains to the dancers the counts for
what they must do, but Nureyev is in there among them,
going up to each group in turn for one maneuver, holding
back its outside dancer until the last moment to prevent
him from starting to turn too soon, then pushing him forward at the crucial second.

After this the atmosphere in the smaller studio is comparatively quiet, even though he is now working once more on the boisterous comic Russian dance. He has gone on to a later section: five couples are whirling rather wildly across the stage, but amid the general melee he immediately spots the one dancer who has gone wrong and is able to tell him how to put it right next time: "Donald, you should get that leg out sooner; it will help get you round and help her."

The men have to jump in among the women. Drew, leading them, asks, "Do you want us to do the jump facing forward or back?" "Whichever is more comfortable at speed." They try it both ways before deciding. During a sequence traveling across the stage, he stops Anderton: "Why have you changed that step?" She explains that there was no time to get around behind Drew. "Then come straight in front." Afterward he gets them to go through the whole dance and draws attention to points of detail in the opening, which yesterday he had let go by, presumably to get them started easily. "Boys, will you please do the first step on demi-pointe, and the whole body should be leaning backwards. The second time you do it, it is already much meeker. Girls, when you pull the boys back, don't look at them; if you take too much notice of them, you won't have time."

Now the three young men who will do the acrobatic, mildly humorous Chinese dance are waiting. When they start, Wayne Eagling does a complicated step, but Nureyev stops him: "No, it's rivoltade." They start again but are again stopped. "You're cheating. I keep my leg straight until I have gone right over and then bring it through." He shows it, and they do the same.

There is a sequence where they bend down in turn and the others roll across their backs. They tend to land for this roll with the small of the back against the supporting one's bottom, but this way they are liable to fall. Tapping the supporting boy's rump, he explains, "You have to put your bum right here, and if you start to fall, he can push up his back to correct it."

They try a sequence when David Ashmole has to do a backward roll off the other boys' backs, fly through the air and land on his feet, and they confirm the way Carl Myers will get his head under Ashmole and lift his shoulders to help give the impetus to start. After this, Eagling does a leap through Myers' encircling arms and lands in a forward roll. Putting Myers straddled in the center, Nureyev jokes: "Now Superman is here, and you both jump on his knees." They try but cannot hold the positions as intended. After a few abortive attempts he decides this must be modified: "Well, I'm sure you are just going to put your leg up and step there, don't jump." They go on to the end. Nureyev decides it would be better if Eagling did an extra pirouette in the finale and less of the mock-Chinese arm movement in which they all join. They run right through the dance. Nureyev points out which of the three it was who had put out one sequence by being late, then decides to call it a day.

He has had something like eight hours' intensive and almost nonstop effort, never relaxing because his eyes must spot whatever goes wrong, his skill must sort it out, his knowledge of the most efficient way of performing every step, for ease or effect, must be passed on. As we leave, he tells me he is off to Paris the next afternoon to see Merce Cunningham's new ballet at the Opéra, on his way to Monte Carlo for the two galas. During the day I have already heard him commit himself to coming into the studio first, to rehearse with both Park and Penney. He does not make things easy for himself, but he gets results.

Talking About Nureyev

NINETTE DE VALOIS
Choreographer and ballet director

I saw *Laurencia* in Leningrad on the night Nureyev made his debut, but he laughs at me and says, "Madame, you don't remember me." I do remember that there were two very good young men in it, because there is another important role for a man, but the names in the program were printed in Russian, of course, and I did not know who they were.

When I first invited him to dance with the Royal Ballet at Covent Garden, there was a lot of criticism from people who thought he was upsetting what had been built up, but my reply at the time was that one must be prepared to risk toppling something over, to find out whether it has been built securely.

It was not the first time we had faced the problem of assimilating a dancer from the Russian school. It happened in 1946, when Violetta Elvin joined us from the Bolshoi Ballet. She too had a completely different approach from that of British dancers, and there had to be adaptations on both sides.

I think the great thing Rudolf taught our dancers was how to expand, but we taught him to put in more detail. You know that the Russians have developed the habit of doing one or two steps, very spectacularly, but missing out the steps in between, just standing or walking around the stage. I told him, "It's no good doing a couple of big jumps and banging the proscenium arch. You have to be able to adapt to different stages, just as a singer must be able to project his voice in differently sized halls."

The Russians are not musically disciplined in the way that our dancers are. When I was in the Diaghilev Ballet, I had to dance a duet with a Russian girl. She would dance it differently every night, but always with a real feeling for the music. We expect that once the choreography is set, it will always be done that way, but the Russian attitude is different. If people say that Nureyev is not musical, they mean that he is not disciplined in his relationship to the music, but I will defend completely his musicality.

When he stops dancing, I think he could become a good choreographer. He has shown in his productions of the classics that he has a very complete knowledge and understanding of these old ballets and an ability to supplement them with dances in the same style. When he mounted *Raymonda*, I told him how beautiful I thought one dance for three girls was, and he said, "It's mine." He is a fine producer; when I saw the Kirov Ballet dance *La Bayadère*, I was disappointed, because that was after he had produced it for the Royal Ballet, and it seemed to me that we danced it better.

I only wish that he did not feel that he has to go everywhere and dance everything. There are plenty of people who can dance these modern roles he does, and while he is concentrating on them, his classical work suffers. I think he should concentrate on what he does better than anyone else, dancing the classics perfectly.

GALINA SAMSOVA
Ballerina

I first heard of Rudi while I was still dancing in Kiev. We had a boy come there from the Kirov School to join the company, and he spoke of this boy in Leningrad who was very talented but supposed to be very undisciplined.

Then I left Russia before he did and went to live in Canada. So I found out for myself that it was not so easy to get work as a dancer in the West after studying in Russia. I tried to get into companies there, just in the corps de ballet, but they said they could not use me because my style was so different that it would look wrong. It was only when Lois Smith, who was ballerina of the National Ballet, was ill that I was asked if I would go to dance some performances she was due to give. And after that I joined the company as one of their ballerinas.

I think for Rudi it was easier for three reasons: because he was a man, and male dancers are scarce; because he was already a principal dancer; and because of the publicity about the way he left. But he has adapted himself in a very clever way since those days, and I think the most important thing that happened to him was meeting Margot. You would not know now, just from seeing him, that he was from the Kirov. There are some things about him that are Kirov, and some things from the Royal Ballet—but mostly it's just him.

ERIK BRUHN
Premier danseur

I first met Rudik when I was dancing in Copenhagen and he came there to take classes with Vera Volkova. The first time we worked together was when I was preparing for my performances with Maria Tallchief. Maria and I wanted to warm up and do class in the afternoon rather than take the regular class in the morning, so that we did not then have a long gap before the performance, and I asked Rudik to join us and give the class. He took everything so slowly and made it so hard that after about a quarter of an hour I had to drop out and say, "I'm sorry, I have a performance, and this will cripple me." This very slow barre work is not something all the Russians do; with Nijinska you were often finished at the barre after five minutes and on to the center work. That's more like the Bournonville school I was brought up in, where there used to be a very short barre, but we have lengthened that because in winter your muscles don't have time to warm up. And when I watched Pushkin's class in Leningrad, some of that was very quick.

But later we worked a lot together and would take it in turns to set the exercises. We got so that we hardly talked at all; we knew and understood each other just from a gesture of the hands. Some photographers once came to take pictures of us in class, and I think they were surprised at the almost total silence. We did not correct each other, even when things went wrong, because we each knew what we were trying to do.

Once he got annoyed when we were working together and said, "It's not like you teaching me; you just look with cold eyes at a body moving, like Balanchine does." I guess I have this way of working, which at the time upset him because it was not his way, but later he came to accept it.

I think we both learned a lot from working together. He is a fantastically hard worker. When we were both performing with the Royal Ballet at Covent Garden in 1962, I had hurt my foot and wanted to strengthen it, and we both used to go to Covent Garden on Sunday when the theater was closed and work for two or three hours each week while everyone else was at home. Without wanting to change each other, I think we both influenced the way the other one did some things.

When he first danced Bournonville, I taught him the *Flower Festival* pas de deux. Because of his different background, he had difficulty with all those small beats. I was delighted to see the solo he had put into *Don Quixote* with all those quick beats, because it showed how he had completely overcome that.

Bournonville was also difficult for him at first because the use of music was so much different from what he had been used to. When Bournonville is using square-cut music, his choreography always goes off the beat and returns later with a bang. He has a special gift for making his choreography fit the music in such a way that to dance it you must have the right music; you cannot do his exercises in class to any old piece of music of similar rhythm. When I was choreographing the Bach piece for our concert, Rudik argued with me about the relationship with the music, but now he never sets anything very squarely with square music, he always varies it.

To work the way he has, traveling from one company to another, needs exceptional self-discipline, because you do not have a permanent artistic director to advise you. Ninette de Valois once told me I was wrong to leave the company where I had been brought up, but I did not split myself up very much, mainly only between the American Ballet Theatre and the Royal Danish Ballet for a lot of the time. Even so, I found that the strain of traveling around as a guest star was a great burden, and every now and again I had to stop and think where I was heading with my career and what I was achieving. Also, I found that I had to drop works from my repertoire for a while simply because I had reached the point where my mind refused to react any longer. It is almost incredible, the way Rudik keeps going on all the time.

I think the most valuable thing I got from him was exactly this drive. When I was very young, dancing in London in 1947 and 1948, there were several dancers around with this quality and talent. I remember seeing Jean Babilée dance Bluebird and wondering why I bothered to try to dance! Then the next day you go to class and work harder than ever because of this example. At that time there was André Eglevsky, too, and a little later Igor Youskevitch. By the time Rudik arrived I had reached a certain eminence, and I was hating the fact of having become established and unable to see where I could progress. His drive and youth and energy helped me to start again in a new way. It is easy to think, "I have enough technique and ability to get through, and something to spare," but when we were working together, we were always trying for something more.

VERA VOLKOVA
Ballet teacher

WHEN Rudi first came to Copenhagen, he was still in his early youth and unsure of the ways of the West, but as a pu-

With Rudi van Dantzig in Amsterdam

In *Monument for a Dead Boy* with the Dutch National Ballet (1968)

Discussing *Petrushka* with Rudi van Dantzig and Toer va Schayk

As Petrushka at the Paris Opera (1975)

As Siegfried in *Swan Lake* (Royal Ballet's 1963 production)

In *Prodigal Son:* leaving home and after being robbed (1973)

As James in *La Sylphide*

in *Sideshow*

3)

Solo in *La Fille mal gardée* (Royal Ballet production, 1974)

In costume for *Don Quixote* (Vienna)

In *The Moor's Pavane*

In costume for *Raymonda,* Act 3 (Australian Ballet)

Drawing by Moira McCaffery

In *Aureole* (New York, 1974)

Solo in *Paradise Lost* (Paris, 1967)

With Carolyn Carlson in *Tristan* (Paris Opera, 1975)

Solo in *Field Figures* (New York, 1972)

As a student, **with** **Galina** Ivanova **and** **Nina** Yastrebova in pas de trois in *Swan Lake*

In *L'Estas* (1968)

Costume adjustment by Rosella Hightower before *La Fille mal gardée* at Marseilles (1962)

As Don Juan (National Ballet of Canada, 1974)

pil he was highly professional, beautifully trained, and I enjoyed teaching him. He took corrections seriously and always gave of his best. Initially, he appeared to be missing his former teacher in Leningrad, Alexander Pushkin, but when he learned that I had in my youth danced with his old master, he was happily reassured.

He has matured as an artist and as a person. He is always well organized, and he plans his career with forethought. It is always a pleasure for a teacher to instruct a great talent, and I feel that we spoke the same language in more senses than one.

FREDERICK ASHTON
Choreographer and ballet director

THE first time the name of Nureyev sprang into my consciousness was in Leningrad with the Royal Ballet, when we heard whispered that he had defected; this was not an easy period for us. On our return we heard of the dramatic incidents that led to his escape and of his triumphs in Paris. Shortly after these events, Fonteyn was organizing one of her RAD galas at Drury Lane and approached me with a view to arranging a dance for Nureyev in which he was to make his London debut. Having heard of his volatile temperament, I was dubious but was won round when I was told that this was his own wish and that, therefore, his willingness would make it easier for us to work together.

He chose the music himself, and I liked it. I had never seen him dance, and I was full of misgivings and trepidations, and on our first meeting we regarded each other with some suspicion. I felt like a ringmaster, wondering if this beautiful animal would perform his tricks or whether I would be mauled in the process. I had possibly never worked with such a brilliant dancer or one of such positive personality. I was not at ease at the first rehearsals, having respect for his superior knowledge of what a male dancer was capable of. We plodded on, and the result was successful. I was aware of what depended on me, and I was really anxious to show him off well and for him to make an instant success. Both happened, and his impact was terrific. Alas, it has never been seen again, but the dance served its purpose, and I am proud that I helped to launch him on the English public, who instantly took him to their hearts as I have taken him to mine.

His intelligence and quickness and avidity of mind are a constant delight, as well as his humor and his desire for more and more knowledge and experience. He goes to see everything in the theater, has a wide interest outside the ballet scene and a wide circle of diverse friends. His mind is always alert, brilliant in interviews although he is thinking in an alien language.

His effect on the Royal Ballet was of inestimable value. He showed the male dancers what their bodies were capable of, and the audacity with which they could present themselves and the excitement they needed to generate. He is also always ready to help other dancers with practical advice as to the best way to execute certain steps stylistically.

I worry that perhaps he extends himself too much in other fields—admirable in a way, but he is, above all, a great classical dancer, and it is through the classics that he provides the great thrills of interpretation and dancing, by investing them with so much life and clarity. Well, I adore him!

MARGOT FONTEYN
Ballerina

I find Nureyev very rewarding to work with. In performance of course he is a forceful stage personality who generates an atmosphere of excitement whenever he dances. In rehearsal he is incredibly hardworking and meticulous in his own dancing and also in helping, explaining or advising generously anyone who cares to learn from him. Very occasionally one can give him a new idea, but his brain is so quick that it is usually way ahead.

NICHOLAS GEORGIADIS
Painter and stage designer

THE first time Rudi asked me to work with him was when he did *Raymonda* for the Royal Ballet touring company in 1964, but at that time I had never designed one of the big classics, and I told him, "No, I have nothing to give you for this." When we eventually did *Raymonda* together in Zurich, he said, "There, you see you can design *Raymonda*," and I replied, "Yes, now I can, but eight years ago I could not."

I did agree to design *Swan Lake* later that year because I was much more familiar with the ballet. But I have an idea that the reason Rudolf wanted me was because I came to these ballets from outside and brought a new eye to them. What I was able to contribute, I think, was a determination to get away from the wishy-washy romantic painted designs and the trompe l'oeil (which nobody can really do now anyway) and to use three-dimensional settings and objects. Rudi has a theory that it is a good thing for the dancers to be contrasted with solid objects onstage, and I think it is true that in these circumstances the dancers seem to be projected forward to the audience, whereas with the painted backcloths the dancers are drawn back into the design.

He likes settings which are rather cavernous and asymmetrical. If I ever show him a sketch which is symmetrical, I can feel straightaway that he is not happy with it, and he starts making suggestions for changes. When we start a collaboration, he gives lots of hints of what he has in mind; he has a strong visual approach. When we did *The Sleeping Beauty,* he visualized the prologue all grays and silvers and black; I was uncertain about this until I realized the effect of contrast he wanted with Aurora's sixteenth birthday in the next act. It was his idea to have the production so architectural. I am not sure whether this was because being Russian he understands the Tchaikovsky music so well or from something he had seen in Russia. He spoke of a marvelous earlier production there, before the present one, where apparently all the costumes looked as if they were really made of heavily embroidered fabrics and then encrusted with stones, but whether he actually saw this or only heard about it I don't know. People have the idea that *The Sleeping Beauty* must be all lightness, they think of the ballet as a *féerie,* and we did not make a *féerie* at all, but I think it works.

Raymonda and *Nutcracker* were the hardest to do; *The Sleeping Beauty* requires the greatest number of designs, but in that and *Swan Lake* the structure of the ballet is clear. With *Raymonda,* by the time I came to do it Rudolf had already staged several versions, so his ideas were well worked out. In *Nutcracker* we have both made a number of changes, first when we revived it at Milan, then rather more in Buenos Aires. I did not go to Buenos Aires myself, but Rudi told me it worked rather well there, so when we revived it again at Covent Garden, we consolidated those changes and made a few more. When you see a work many times onstage, sometimes you realize that something you thought essential is not really necessary at all, so we cut it out. For the latest Covent Garden revival we did not have to make any new structures, only to eliminate some and change the way we used others, but I think even if you have to spend money to improve a production, it's worth it. It is significant that Rudi goes on working on his productions all the time, always trying to make them better.

He has the ability to read a design, which not everyone can do, and know what it will look like, although perhaps sometimes in a rather literal way. If I drew a simplified or distorted sketch for a costume, he might object that he cannot visualize how it will look on the stage, and in fact, I think he was right; I always attempt to draw the proportions of the figures more or less realistic. And when the costumes are made up, he sees at once if perhaps there is too much contrast or a color wrong. Sometimes as the designer you are not sure whether to change a color or spray a costume, and it is a great help to have an eye like his that really sees.

I suppose it is partly because of coming from another tradition that he questions things which we take for granted. Sometimes he will ask *why* you do something, even quite basic. And he sees everything, all the shows. I think this is very important for a producer, to be well informed. Also, he has a marvelous gift of phrase. I remember for instance when rehearsing the Canadian *Sleeping Beauty*, Carabosse's monsters are supposed to force the courtiers from the table where they have been eating, but the courtiers ran away too soon, when they saw the monsters coming, and he took the microphone and said, "You must abandon your places with more discomfort." That I think was an amazing way to put it.

MARCIA HAYDÉE
Ballerina

I love working with Rudolf. He has the reputation of being difficult and complicated, but I suppose all artists are complicated, and most of us can be difficult sometimes. With him, just because it is Nureyev, and because of all the publicity he has had, people make a big thing of it. I have never had any difficulty at all when I have worked with him.

We spent a month working on *Raymonda,* and I enjoyed it so much. I am sure it was good for me to dance a role like that, with six solos, three pas de deux and a pas de sept. You have to work fantastically hard because he expects it. Anyone who does not work hard he has no time for. He made me do all sorts of things I thought I could not do, and he was so helpful. Somehow by sheer willpower you manage to cope, and I think that, ever since, I have been better able to cope with things because of that experience.

The first time we danced together was at Covent Garden, in *Das Lied von der Erde,* just one performance. Then it was such a surprise, one day here in Stuttgart the telephone rang and a voice said, "It's Rudolf; would you like to come and dance *Swan Lake* with me in Zurich?" It was so unexpected—he has all these girls he could choose from, and he asks me! But I think it was very good for me. He takes me with him to these places, and we have two days' rehearsal, perhaps only one, no stage call, no rehearsal with the com-

166

pany or the orchestra, and a different version of the ballet. It made me find a new way of working.

And as a person, as a friend he is so wonderful. If he does not like somebody, he makes it very clear, and he has a manner to keep people at a distance, which I suppose is just a protection, because people push him all the time, and he has to fight them off or he would not get any peace at all. But if he likes you, once you penetrate beneath the surface, he is very warm and will take any trouble, and you know you can rely upon him absolutely.

RUDI VAN DANTZIG
Choreogapher and ballet director

IT was Rudolf's own suggestion to come and dance *Monument for a Dead Boy* with the Dutch National Ballet. He had not seen it, but friends had told him about it, and he thought it might be something interesting for him to do. He was dancing in Amsterdam with the Royal Ballet and made an appointment through someone else for me to go and see him. I had never met him, and when I went to his dressing room, he was making up. I saw those keen eyes looking at me sideways in the mirror, very sharply—like a fox. When he said what he was thinking of, I did not really believe anything would come of it; I thought perhaps it was just a whim. But then he telephoned me afterward, and I realized that he meant it.

Even then I thought it would be a long time, perhaps a year, but it all happened in just a few months. When he arrived to learn the ballet, the company was away somewhere performing; just one girl had remained behind of those he would have to dance with, so I began by teaching him a pas de deux. I was glad to start quietly like this, because I was terrified: I had never worked with someone as distinguished as this. But it all went well; only I had not a clue to what he thought about working with us or about the choreography he was learning. Although we spoke, almost every evening of his week's stay, about the part of the boy in *Monument*, the background and the motivations of the role, he never really said what his opinion of the whole enterprise was. He was just being very careful with words, I think.

The second day, when the company returned, they all treated him very warmly, not at all distantly (I think perhaps this is rather a Dutch attitude), so there was a happy atmosphere. I was astonished how quickly he learned and how well he got along with dancers totally unknown to him. Learning to know him was like being taken by an avalanche; his speed in learning new steps and ideas, his greed for always newer things, his energy once he was going, his many interests, not only in dance but in theater, film, exhibitions, are amazing. I will always remember our walks through Amsterdam after performances, he in enormous coat and fur hat, protected from the cold, strolling through empty streets, looking at antique shops while he told me about his youth in Ufa, memories of fishing holidays with his father, his first lonely arrival in Leningrad and the years with his beloved teacher Pushkin.

That time with us he danced just *Monument* and a pas de deux from *The Nutcracker.* He insisted on doing this because he said the audience must see him do something classical in the same program. Later he came back and danced Apollo and Petrushka. His Apollo was for me, besides *Giselle,* one of the most beautiful things he danced with us. The growing strength of a stumbling, newborn but already powerful being into a shining, radiant god was in perfect counterbalance with the elegant quicksilver variations of the three muses, and throughout the work you could feel and see the inspiration and perfection rise and rise in his being up to the climax of the ballet, where he triumphantly leaves the earth and is brought up to heaven.

As for Petrushka, it was the first time I realized how Russian the ballet is. So much of the tragedy of Russian history is in that character. Rudolf told us he had not been happy when he danced the part before, and he worked on it in very great detail, especially with Toer van Schayk, who was the régisseur for that production. Toer is a great Russophile, and all this came out, I think. For me, Rudolf was so marvelous in rehearsal that onstage it was a slight disappointment: there was so much expression in his face, which was less clear when he had makeup on, and he had a costume sent from Covent Garden which looked too bright and new. We told him it should be more ragged and dirty, but I don't think he really believed us. However, when he was dancing with us later, he would ask, "Does that look all right?" and he said to me, "If you don't like my costume or what I do, you must say and I will change it, because you are the director."

When the Kirov Ballet was in London, I arranged a—rather secretive—meeting between Rudolf and one of the dancers who appeared to be a former classmate of his. We went to dinner where many memories were to be talked about and information about the latest happenings in Leningrad exchanged. The old school friend asked Rudolf if he ever regretted having left Russia, his friends, family and colleagues, but Rudolf answered that he lived for dancing and that in the West he could dance whatever he liked, any style, modern as well as classic, and as often as he wanted to. That for him was the important thing.

It was a very good thing for me to have the chance to

work with him, and for the company, too. I hope one day we can do another new production together; he has said he would be interested, but I need time to create a new ballet, and it is not easy to fit in the dates when we are free with the times when he is available.

When I made *Ropes of Time* at Covent Garden, that also was at his suggestion, I think. He had to have something new for the American tour. He told me then it was the first time a ballet had been created just for him, and he seemed anxious about how long he would be onstage and whether he would have enough variations. He said he hoped the leading part was not going to be like the one in *Monument,* what he called a passive, observative role. On the contrary, he wanted it to be very active and involved in all the action.

I was nervous, too, creating a work outside my own company, and in the rehearsal room we would sometimes have an explosion. But then afterward he would come to me in the dressing room and say, "Let's go out and eat." With most people I find that if there is some kind of dispute, it goes on for days, but he is able to cut himself right off from it as soon as it is over and be completely warm and natural.

This was one of the pleasures of working with him, the contact with this very warm, human person. When he first worked with us, he came to stay with Toer and myself in our house in Amsterdam. It is very small and simple, and the spare room is tiny with a not too comfortable bed in it, but he accepted it all quite naturally and was at once one of the family. When *Ropes* was done in London, my parents and Toer's parents were over, and he treated them very kindly and made sure they felt at ease, as he did for everyone else when he gave a big party for the entire cast of *Ropes* after the first night. I later met his mother and sister in Leningrad. The likeness with his mother one could see at once. She had many pictures of him, including recent ones, and I brought her some more. But apparently all she wanted was news about her son. Alas, there is the terrible barrier of language, and I fear I failed in giving her what she wanted so badly.

When we were working on *Ropes,* he was very concerned about dancing it in the right style. He came to me and said we could hire a studio and go on working on it in the evening after rehearsals and on Sundays. He works so hard I don't know how he keeps it up.

When *Ropes* was finished, I had the awful feeling I had not really given him the ballet he deserved and had hoped for. He, however, was so full of praise and happiness about it that it made me happy as well; it was very beautiful to hear him speak in detail about the choreography. It was not a mere vehicle for him to shine in, but it was the construction of the ballet as a whole, the themes in movement, the time and tide in emotions through the steps that intrigued him most.

The beginning and end of the ballet: Rudolf as a tiny lonely figure on a blue globe in the wide empty space of Covent Garden stage, emperor and subject at the same time. That is how I very often see and think of him: emperor to the audience, subject to Terpsichore.

MAURICE BÉJART
Choreographer and ballet director

NUREYEV learns very quickly because he has an exceptional intelligence and he also has an exceptional instinct. One half of him is a wonderfully well organized person, with everything analyzed and under control, but the other half of him is like a creature groping in the dark, doing everything by touch and by smell. It is the combination of these qualities which makes him what he is. That is why he can do anything, absolutely anything that he really wants to do.

MAINA GIELGUD
Ballerina

THE first time I danced with Rudi was in Rosella Hightower's production of *The Sleeping Beauty* in Barcelona. I was with Béjart's company at the time, and he let me off to dance my first Aurora at very short notice: just four days in Barcelona after two days in Marseilles to learn and rehearse it—and only the last two with Rudi! But in those two days he taught me so much about how to present oneself in classical roles. He inspected my tutus, flattened my headdress—and when we were half dead, he made us laugh.

A thing I remember is that after one performance people were already coming backstage while we were taking calls. They were standing at the side watching, and I found it rather horrifying. I said to Rudi, "That woman is looking at you as if you were an animal in a zoo," and he answered, "I am."

The next time I worked with him was in Marseilles when he mounted *Don Quixote*. That was an incredible experience, to see the way he worked. He would rehearse from morning until early evening with the company, then stay until late at night working on his own role. He was adding some new choreography, too, including that duet at the beginning of Act 2, and I was very proud because he worked it out with me. What would probably surprise most people is that all the time he wanted to know what other people who were there thought of it. "Does that look OK?" he would ask, when he had worked out something. Once he dried out and couldn't find the next enchainement—that was well after midnight—so he knelt down, looked up at the sky, half frowning, half joking, and begged, "Please—help!" And out *did* come the next step!

He is a marvelous person to work with because he can spot the essential things. A good ballet master can usually tell you a whole list of things that need correcting, but I find that you then have to work out for yourself what to concentrate on, that will help your particular performance. Rudi will tell you just one or two things that make it all clear. Also, the way he counts a musical phrase, the way he emphasizes the rhythm and the beat, gives one immediately the right attack toward the enchainement.

Many ballet masters are good when working with perhaps three or four people, up to about eight or ten at most, but there are very few who are equally good with a large corps de ballet. Rudi has this rare gift to look at a corps, perhaps fifty dancers, and spot the ones he should concentrate on to get an improvement.

You know that he has this habit, before a performance, of practicing every difficult step he is going to have to do, until he gets it exactly right. Most of us could never do that. If a step is especially difficult, one tends to rely on the heat of the performance to get one through it. But he will even make them hold the curtain, if necessary, until he is satisfied. It is incredible how conscientious he is.

If something goes wrong during a performance, he has a trick of seeming to switch off and withdraw. Obviously it is his way of coping with the situation, but it can be terrifying if you are dancing with him. But it is always exhilarating to dance with him. Apparently someone in the audience (a Licéo balletomane) was heard to remark, "I'd rather have Nureyev on an 'off' day than any other dancer on his 'on' day!"

The other amazing thing about him is the way he deliberately gives himself such difficult things to do all the time. He could so easily get away with doing just one or two things that look spectacular but actually are not too hard, and very few people would know the difference. He has to make it really hard for himself, a perpetual, burning challenge to go further.

DAVID WALL
Premier danseur

RUDOLF arrived in the West when I was still a student, and even then he was a tremendous inspiration. I had hardly seen any ballet until I left the Royal Ballet School at Richmond and joined the senior students at Baron's Court. The performances of his which I saw were inspiring, and so was working in the same building as him. Even through the glass door of a studio one became aware of his—dedication is not really the word I want, but his energy could be felt. He has immense concentration and power, a kind of physical dedication. The two biggest influences on me at that stage of my career were Rudolf and John Field when he was directing the Royal Ballet's touring company.

When I joined the company, the first time I worked with Rudolf was when he came to mount *Raymonda*. There were some tensions, but they did not worry me, and the experience was enjoyable, for me and, I think, for everybody in the company, because he made the work so exciting and fulfilling and in this way got good results. At that time he danced Jean de Brienne, and I was just in the Grand Pas Hongrois. Later, when we mounted the last act on its own, I danced the lead. I had to come to London to learn it while the company was on tour. Valentina Pereyaslavec, the teacher Rudolf always goes to in New York, had been invited to London at that time, and I worked on it with her as well as with Rudolf. I think he was genuinely pleased that I danced the role and had a success in it. He is not at all jealous and likes to help other dancers to do well if they have any talent and have a will to work. Envious of some things, maybe; we all are, even Rudolf, but not jealous. He will always help any dancer who asks him, and I have a feeling that any problem I had, professionally, a decision to take or whatever, I could always go to him and get an honest answer.

I learned something from him, too, indirectly, when I first partnered Margot. I was very new then; I think it was the first time she had danced with someone so young, and she would sometimes say, "Rudolf finds it easier to do it this way," and of course, I took that advice. But I have never tried to imitate him and dance his way. I don't do everything the way he does, and sometimes if we are rehearsing, I will say, "I would rather not do that; I feel more comfortable doing this." He does not mind at all.

When he first mounted *The Nutcracker,* I was still with the touring company and came in just to dance two performances. That was not such a good time for me, because I was not there all through the rehearsals and I was working with a company I was not used to. But the latest time of doing *Nutcracker* was enjoyable, working on the new pas de deux.

We have had some good times together, especially on

tour. I think people don't realize what a marvelous sense of humor he has. And it was great fun working with him in *Dances at a Gathering*. You know, when he is in London, the programs have to be arranged so that he has several performances close together, and that leaves fewer performances for the rest of us—but I miss him when he is not around.

Looking at Nureyev

THERE is one aspect of Nureyev's dancing which has hardly ever been mentioned, yet almost everyone who has seen him often must be aware of it, and it is one of the most engaging things about him. I am thinking of the fact that often you can still see, inside the famous star, that small boy in Ufa who danced for the sheer joy of it. It shows especially whenever he performs pas de chat (that step where, to put it in nontechnical terms, he jumps sideways, tucking his legs up beneath him). Every time he does this a kind of glee comes into his dancing; his eyes sparkle, and the step takes on an almost giggling quality. You can easily imagine the urchin, so disreputable in the eyes of his father and his teachers, about whom school reports said, "He jumps like a frog, and that's about all he knows. He even dances on the staircase landings." The joyousness, the ability to transmit to an audience the sheer delight of dancing, is part of him, and an important part.

In another respect, too, the boy is still there in the man. The fierce ambition that stopped him from giving up when every hope seemed doomed, the constant quest toward an unreachable ideal of perfection, the bravado enabling him to dance a solo he had never learned—those qualities are still there, burning inside, providing his drive. He has a more powerful engine than other dancers. Ashton said after first working with him that he was "like a Rolls-Royce. You could feel his power when he started up at rehearsals." And, like a Rolls, it is not only that he can go fast and strong and continue longer; he also has, when he wants it, the quietness, the smoothness, the gentle control.

Then there is the total involvement in whatever he is doing. Another great dancer, Anna Pavlova, thought that it was a specifically Russian quality to be able to "surrender himself so completely to his art," but it would be more accurate to say that the sort of involvement a Pavlova or Nureyev shows is something personal, not national. In any case, Nureyev insists, rightly, that he is a Tartar, not a Russian. In his autobiography he wrote: "I can sense the difference in my flesh. Our Tartar blood runs faster somehow, it is always ready to boil. And yet it seems to me that we are more languid than the Russians, more sensuous; we have a certain Asiatic softness in us. . . . We are a curious mixture of tenderness and brutality—a blend which rarely exists in the Russian (perhaps that is why I discover such a strong affinity with many of Dostoevsky's characters). Tartars are quick to catch fire, quick to get into a fight, unassuming, yet at the same time passionate and sometimes cunning as a fox. The Tartar is in fact a pretty complex animal."

That complexity is another of the attributes making up his character onstage and off. It gives richness to his work; you can never take him for granted or know exactly what to expect, nor is he often content to operate on just one level at a time. There are any number of aspects of him, all absolutely characteristic. Look at his photographs; see how different he looks from one to another. It is more than a matter of being cheerful in one, stern in another, now concentrating, now relaxed. The shape of the face seems to change, the whole body takes on a different balance and tension. Yet he is always recognizable. In *Don Quixote* at one point he changes costume, covers his face with an enormous bushy beard, and gets busy arranging the curtains around the little stage on a handcart where the gypsies are to put on a show. Even then you could hardly for a moment mistake him for anyone else.

The gift of being always the character, yet always himself is something he shares with certain great actors. Sir Laurence Olivier is one who springs to mind. It is many years since Olivier performed a famous double bill of *Oedipus* and *The Critic*, but it remains in many memories a highlight of his career. The idea was to show off his range, from the dark power and depth of Greek tragedy to Sheridan's quick, foppish, puffball comedy. Few other actors could have come near his level in either role, and nobody would have dared challenge him in both. Yet although the two parts were perfectly embodied with a complete change of style, manner, voice and appearance between the two plays, in each one was aware not only of the character but of Olivier's concept of the character. Similarly with Nureyev: on those ambitiously varied triple bills he loves to dance, where he shows three contrasted styles and characters in a single night, he embodies and expresses the different works in a way that vividly reveals their essential qualities, but never himself becomes anonymous or transparent in doing so.

I think this offers an insight into one of the qualities distinguishing a star from other performers. Often we may go to the theater for the sake of the play or ballet or opera that is being performed, but there are times when we are drawn there specifically for a particular performance. We may say not just that we are going to see *Hamlet,* but to see Gielgud's or Scofield's or whoever's Hamlet. And the quality we are looking for in those circumstances is not so much identification or technical perfection or even originality, although all those qualities are important, but the vital gift is illumination.

When Nureyev first arrived in the West, he already had that, like his other talents, in embryo. He came with glowing accounts of what he had already achieved in the Soviet Union. Advance publicity for the Kirov Ballet's visit singled him out for special mention: "extraordinary" he was called, and we were told that much was expected of him. But his style was still unformed. He had, I think, a clear idea of what he wanted to do, but probably not yet how to do it—or if he had the knowledge, he had not yet the full mastery. The dancer we saw then was in some ways more thrilling than any other, but capable of some awful moments, too. The faults were almost certainly more conspicuous than they would have been in other dancers, partly because of the wholeheartedness with which he did everything, partly because his presence onstage made everyone unusually attentive. That was not only the result of publicity making people concentrate on him; his personality also acted as a focusing lens.

Consequently, some people seemed able to notice only the way he sometimes bumped on landing from jumps, while others were admiring the height to which he leaped. I wonder whether any of us were as conscious as we should have been of the careful way he showed off that height to best advantage. The angle of a leg or arm, both in the air and on landing, is crucial in this, also the timing and trajectory of the jump. The consciousness of how a step works is something Nureyev has developed to a high pitch. Plenty of dancers who have worked with him remark on the fact that he can tell you just how the muscles have to be used to get the effect needed, the timing necessary and where the weight must fall. When he rehearses, it is the attempt at perfect execution of the steps that he concentrates on.

However, that is not simply for virtuosity's sake. Even in a pure dancing role he looks for the essential character of that particular dance. You can see this in his *Corsair* pas de deux, and the way his performance developed over the years brings it out more clearly. When he danced it at twenty-three, we were so dazzled by the soaring way he corkscrewed into the air in his solo and the wide high arc of his leaps in the coda that it was difficult to take in much else. A decade later the dancing is still strong and clear, but no longer bursting with the first radiance of youth. I am not trying to hint that nowadays he dances the role badly. In fact, he is still better than anyone else I have seen in it, and even by comparison with his younger self the only loss is that bonus of freshness which the years must take away. That ought to mean some falling off in excitement, but in some respects his performance is more thrilling than ever, thanks to the way he interprets instead of merely executing steps. When he runs across the stage before his solo, he goes straight and fast like an arrow, then stops and draws himself up into an arabesque, which he holds for a moment as taut as a bowstring. So even before he starts to dance, he has projected an image of attack, sharpness, tension, thus giving an extra edge to everything that follows. I doubt whether he has these literary ideas in mind (although it is not impossible), but the physical effect he intends and achieves is unmistakable.

His dancing always had a strong line to it, but that line

was not always so boldly drawn as now. He had a body with muscles that could achieve sensational results, he had a compelling personality, a feeling for style and an aura of glamor. But those qualities sometimes played around a role, even I think with Albrecht in *Giselle,* his first big role in London and one of his greatest successes. The very boyish way of standing, the impetuousness, the aristocratic manner—these were convincing from the start. Outstanding, too, was the quality of his dancing, the almost sensuous smoothness, the way he not only soared apparently to shoulder height in his cabrioles, but seemed positively to scorn the ground. Always he has moved on a big scale; he dislikes small stages, and on a big stage he uses the whole of it, being impatient with the way so many dancers tend to keep near the middle. "That way, you don't see diagonals and circles and other floor patterns which make the dance more interesting," he says. "People seem to think that if you go to the side, nobody watches."

But although his Albrecht already had those virtues, in early days he also had a habit of decorating the role with some soft, florid arm movements which seemed empty by comparison with the purposeful nature of most of his gestures. These he has eliminated, cutting away anything extraneous to the character and thus projecting the drama more forcefully. I have already mentioned the extra solo Nureyev invented for Albrecht, the series of entrechats which many others have copied since. Like many of Nureyev's innovations, it horrified many people at first but has come to be accepted for its logic, helping to tell the story more clearly, not just to show off a brilliant technique.

Equally horrifying to many people at first was the new solo he invented for Siegfried. Erik Bruhn told me that he and Nureyev, discussing the character, came simultaneously to the thought that a solo was needed at this early point in the action, to help establish the mood of melancholy, and that it could be fitted to one of the dances available in the score but generally not used. They each choreographed their own version on similar lines, using the steps of classical dancing for an unusually introspective mood. Both the choice of music and the style of movement were startling for a man's solo, much more gentle and quiet than would have been thought fitting by Western choreographers, who were still concerned to overcome the widespread misconception of male dancing as somehow effeminate. Nobody ever leveled that charge at Bruhn or Nureyev, so they were able to introduce this softer style which has since been taken up by others in appropriate contexts (many recent productions of *The Sleeping Beauty* give the Prince such a solo, for instance). For someone still very new to choreography to risk such an innovation was bold.

Daring was a quality Nureyev never lacked. All through his career he has forced himself to attempt difficult things. Most star dancers have a few roles in which they specialize and a number of favorite steps which they do particularly well and like to introduce at every opportunity. Nijinsky's fame, for instance, was based almost exclusively on the roles created to exploit his wonderful qualities. In classical roles he was seen less often and less successfully, and photographs confirm the Leningrad tradition which Nureyev once mentioned to me, that his extraordinarily developed thigh muscles gave him poor line. Leonide Massine became a star by creating a gallery of eccentric characters for himself. In more recent years Jean Babilée shone mainly in heavily dramatic parts, Vladimir Vassiliev has been confined by the somewhat limited repertory of the Bolshoi Ballet, and although Edward Villella has tried to vary his

183

staple diet of Balanchine works from the New York City Ballet's repertory, his excursions have taken him mainly into the standard classics. Bruhn danced a varied repertory, from the old classics to dramatic roles, sometimes by comparatively untried choreographers, but he limited the number of works he undertook at any time. I am not condemning these dancers, all of them men of unusual talent, but only trying to demonstrate how unusual it is for Nureyev continually to go from one style to another within the course of a single week, even a single evening.

Even within the classical style which was his starting point and remains his point of reference, he is less restricted than almost any rival. He cannot do everything equally well, but he has constantly widened his range. Russian training, so good at developing a strong jump and flexible back, is generally less suited to developing tiny, neat steps: he has kept his Russian strength and suppleness while adding a Western meticulousness. The best Western dancers can excel most Russians in a grand pirouette by the height to which they lift their leg (parallel to the floor) and the speed they attain; Nureyev still cannot quite match the best of them at this, but he comes close to it. Every dancer turns more happily in one direction than the other, but where the role demands it, he turns alternate ways equally well. Always he stretches himself, and if you watch closely the solos in his own productions, you will see that each introduces a different selection of steps.

That is one way in which he makes things hard for himself, but there is another, more obvious. You have only to think of the way he cleaves the air in *Corsair*, the hurtling leaps of *Bayadère*, Armand's impulsively twisting solo with the whip, the cabrioles which seem to get higher on each repetition in *Raymonda* or any number of other examples to visualize the sheer impetuousness he brings to his dancing. This is one end of his range, and the quiet, fingertip control at the other extreme is just as important, but I am sure that it is this physical bravado which in most people's minds is linked with the name Nureyev. The risk with this is that you may come a cropper, but the thoroughness with which he prepares every role ensures that he achieves his feats of courage as successfully as others manage their more limited aim. Consequently, his dancing has a quality of excitement which is thrilling to watch. He has said that waiting in the wings for his entrance, he is terrified, but once onstage his body can "burst into flames."

But the excitement generated by his performances does not come only from that. He has to an exceptionally high degree the quality that distinguishes some theatrical artists (actors and singers as well as dancers) of being able to command attention immediately by his presence rather than any particular action. He has only to walk onstage and before he dances a step the audience feels a sense of tension that persists to enforce concentration on whatever follows. Obviously his reputation alone would cause something of the sort, but there is more to it than that. Partly it springs from having a strong personality and the ability to project it, but partly also from his air of complete concentration. Since Fonteyn also has this quality to a notable degree, their appearance together always has an electrifying effect.

The musical understanding which is another important element in his success is more difficult to define. It is even sometimes suggested, simply because his phrasing is different from British dancers, that he is not particularly musical. I have already quoted Ninette de Valois on that topic; the most extreme example of the distinction she makes came when he danced *Symphonic Variations.* It is easy to

185

understand the objection that Ashton's choreography provides so sensitive an interpretation of César Franck's music that the way he has set it must be followed meticulously. Nureyev performed the choreography correctly but at the same time looked for his own understanding of the music. If it was wrong, it was gloriously wrong, and the remarkable thing is that it was possible to discuss his performance in musical terms (maestoso, giubiloso and so on) more easily than in purely balletic terms.

In *Les Sylphides,* another ballet depending on the relationship of dance and music more than any other factor, he told a friend that he took his interpretation entirely from the Chopin pieces, ignoring any previous conceptions of the right style or mood. That explains why his performance is so satisfying and avoids any hint of sentimentality. Another Chopin ballet, with a greater variety of moods, is *Dances at a Gathering.* The solo he dances at the beginning of the ballet has to be quiet and understated, seeming to draw the first notes from the pianist by the way he sketches a movement with his feet. The ending, too, is subdued: standing still, crouching and pressing his hand to the floor in an ambiguous but emotional gesture. In between he has a set of flirtatious mazurkas, a jesting dance competition with Anthony Dowell, a Harlequin-like duet with Antoinette Sibley, a swirling solo to the only piece of music in the whole ballet that is not basically in three-quarter time. Each entry catches the spirit as well as the shape and pace of the music: lightly gamboling in one dance, gravely affectionate in another; now driving hard, now light and precise, now gentle and easy.

It is not often, unfortunately, that we have the chance to see him dance as one of a team of equals, as he does in this ballet. Managements understandably want to cast him in big starring roles. But even when playing the romantic heroes, Nureyev looks for a lively response from other dancers around him (as Albrecht, for instance, he makes more intelligible than usual the mime conversations with his squire, Wilfrid). Given the chance of relating on equal terms to other dancers of real quality, as happens in *Dances at a Gathering,* the play of personality becomes especially rewarding.

This work reveals, too, Nureyev's similarities to and differences from the British dancers. When Anthony Dowell takes the opening solo, for instance, he dances it equally well, with a light deft style, but he does not give it the feeling of weightiness Nureyev achieves. It is the quality which sculptors call mass. That is something Nureyev has developed over the years. When he first came to the West, he looked very slight in build; now he has tremendously powerful shoulders. Yet the effect is never heavy or dragging, rather one of strength and force, revealing the muscularity and power of the dance. Apart from its benefit to the texture of the dance, there is the advantage that a man of powerful build leaping through the air is always more impressive than one of slighter physique.

That and his individual response to music are what differentiate Nureyev from the other dancers in *Dances at a Gathering;* what he shares with them is a tendency to bring out the hints of character and humor implicit in Robbins' choreography. Spectators familiar with the original American cast of *Dances* have complained at what they see as an attempt to make up a story where none exists. But there is no question of the Royal Ballet cast's having altered the choreography, and if they added anything, it was only their own characters, their own response to movement and situation. That is a characteristic of British dancing, and Nureyev's own strong inclination in that direction helped him to fit especially well into the Royal Ballet which, although the number of his performances has been limited in any one season, has remained over the years the base to which he constantly returns between his activities elsewhere.

Nureyev always had the idea that without character, dancing is nothing. I do not mean that every role has to portray a character in the sense that a dramatist uses the word, but that every dance, even in a plotless work, must have its own distinctive style and quality—in other words, a character of its own. When he first danced in London, he gave a television interview in which he was asked about his approach to ballets like *Swan Lake* or *Giselle* and replied, "I think there's a way of using old choreography. . . . You are obliged to find a basis for each movement, and without this it could have no truth. You cannot move around the stage doing any one gesture or any one piece of mime. You believe through your whole movement—otherwise, it is immediately seen by audience and everybody that it's wrong." He was less fluent in English then, but I think the idea is clear enough, and as Nureyev explained at the time, it was based on Stanislavsky's methods. But he took the idea beyond Stanislavsky's search for dramatic truth, into a search for musical and choreographic truth. That is why even a classical solo, when he dances it, is never purely abstract; it takes on qualities of sharpness or softness, tautness or relaxation, aggression, humor, sorrow, according to its shape, coloring and context.

That is not simply an instinctive response on his part to the steps and the music, but the result of a conscious wish to know how things work, to discover structure and purpose. That comes out also in his productions of the classics, where he always has a point of view to start from. For instance, his *Swan Lake* is built on the idea that the Prince is the central character, with Odette and Odile simply part of his experience. That does not mean that the ballerina has any less than usual to do, but the story is pulled sharply into focus by seeing it through one pair of eyes.

With *Raymonda,* having decided that the heroine must be the motivator of the action, he went to the extent of deliberately making the hero an insipid character at first, noble but uninspiring. Thus, the dream sequences (which he considerably extended) become an expression of Raymonda's thoughts about her approaching marriage, her unconscious wish that Jean de Brienne should be more like his dark, sinister adversary Abderachman. Not until she can see Jean as a heroic warrior, and in her own mind identify the two opposing characters, is she ready for marriage. This interpretation makes sense at last of a plot which, ever since the ballet's first production in 1898, had seemed confused and feeble and had been tolerated only for the merits of Glazunov's music and Petipa's choreography.

This psychological reinterpretation of *Raymonda* suggests a more intellectual approach than one expects in the production of classic ballets, but it needs no conscious understanding from the audience since it makes emotional and dramatic sense without needing explanation. It is noteworthy that the solution came only on Nureyev's third attempt at the work. In his two previous stagings he had stripped away the plot's less satisfactory features; finally came this fresh reading. His willingness to go on rethinking and reshaping his conception of a work, rare among his contemporaries, is one of his strengths.

What the three versions had in common was Petipa's choreography as their basis. In particular, Petipa created a marvelous role for the ballerina, with many interesting and varied solos. Nureyev kept these and even added to them, applying to the rest of the ballet the same principles as an architect restoring a house fallen into disrepair. What was still good he preserved, and where replacement was needed he tried to follow a style that would fit with the rest. For instance, *Raymonda* contains one of the few display dances Petipa created for men, the pas de quatre in the last act. Originally, I believe, that was the hero's only chance to display his prowess. Nowadays it would seem odd to have the leading man dance only as one of a group, and I know of no recent production where Jean takes part in this quartet. Either he appears only as a partner (as in the Bolshoi's production of this act) or he has a new solo invented for him. That was Nureyev's choice, using music from earlier in the ballet. But he has set Jean's dances in an academic style which looks right in the context of Petipa's dances for the heroine and her friends. Because Nureyev has not merely learned the traditional choreography but analyzed its structure and methods, he can invent new dances in the same style.

When Nureyev undertook his first big productions, the general failure to appreciate initially how much new choreography he was creating came largely because *Raymonda* was unfamiliar in the West. It was easy to assume that he must know it thoroughly from his Russian days and needed only to teach it, making a few amendments here and there. But with that and *Swan Lake,* within three months of each other in 1964, he was undertaking his first large-scale ventures into choreographic creation, teaching himself the job in front of fellow dancers and audiences with none of the usual workshop experiments or apprentice period first.

The Vienna *Swan Lake* was not entirely satisfactory, although it has proved long-lived. If he were to mount the ballet afresh, Nureyev would certainly make many changes, as he did with *Raymonda*. But what a wealth of confidence it showed to invent all those bravura dances for the first act, to adapt the national dances of Act 3 so boldly and to make a version of the last act which, although Cranko had anticipated some aspects of it, was still revolutionary in its tragic emphasis.

In the early versions of *Raymonda* you could see more clearly the strengths and limitations of his choreography. When it came to staging a solo, he never had any trouble at all. He enjoys the gift not just of stringing steps together, but thanks to his assiduous study of the craft (above all, in taking as his model the pure classicism of Petipa's ballets), of giving them harmony and a logical shape. Surprisingly often, even in his early attempts, he could go further and give a virtuoso solo the special flavor or distinctive characteristics which made it reveal something about the role rather than just embellishing it; the heroic assertiveness of Jean's dances in the last act of *Raymonda* is an example

He also showed from the beginning a remarkable confidence in handling large groups. This is a skill which many choreographers take years to acquire (some, indeed, seem never to gain it). The way the corps de ballet whirl in and out of the big waltzes in *Raymonda* is a joy to watch. Sometimes Nureyev goes in for a rather monumental patterning for the ensemble; this, he told me, is because he had observed that Petipa used a heavier style on occasions to show off by contrast a more spectacular dance that was to follow.

Where he did seem to have difficulty at first was in the composition of duets. In his early treatments of *Raymonda*, they sometimes tended to look more like two concurrent solos. It was easy to understand that he wanted to emancipate the male dancer and give him more to dance than had been acceptable when the ballet was first written, but the result was not happy, especially when matched against Glazunov's voluptuous love music. Later he overcame that tendency and taught himself to compose real duets while still giving both dancers their due share of attention.

Nowhere can that be seen better than in his *Nutcracker*. This is probably the most frequently performed of all ballets, partly because of the attraction of Tchaikovsky's music, partly because it is thought especially suitable for children and as a Christmas treat and also because the simple story and surprisingly loose basic structure of the drama make it easily adaptable to the resources of amateur or semiprofessional companies. Consequently, *The Nutcracker* has tended to be a ballet popular with the general public but regarded by ballet lovers as rather a bore. Many attempts have been made over the years to strengthen the plot or to emphasize the dance interest of the many divertissements. Apart from George Balanchine's child-oriented production in New York and a couple of productions in Germany which used the familiar music for a completely different plot, the most successful attempts at breathing new life into *The Nutcracker*, among Nureyev's immediate predecessors, had probably been those of Frederick Ashton and Yuri Grigorovich. Ashton's completely plotless production for the Royal Ballet in 1951 had omitted the first two scenes and presented the dances from the rest of the ballet as a spectacular entertainment. Grigorovich presented the whole story at the Bolshoi in 1966 as a child's dream of growing up. Grigorovich's inspiration was probably the earlier Russian production by Vassily Vainonen which Nureyev acknowledges as his starting point, too. Where they differ is in motivation and style. Grigorovich introduces a new character, a comic conjurer with mystical overtones,

to set the child's dream in motion, and he sees all the enter-
tainers who perform the display dances of the final scene as
dolls come to life. All this is shown in a cozy style, like a
Russian cartoon version of Biedermeier.

Nureyev, on the one hand, sticks closer to the original
plot, retaining the traditional character Drosselmeyer, an
eccentric friend of the family whose party tricks cause Clara's imagination to start racing. But he transforms the situation by identifying Drosselmeyer with Clara's dream prince
and showing almost all the other dream figures as members
of her family in different guises, thus giving a psychological
interest to the drama. Also, he makes no bones about using
all the resources of a big stage and a large company, thus
achieving a grandeur matching Tchaikovsky's music better
than rival productions. When he uses a corps de ballet of
children in the opening Christmas party scene, he brings
them on in neat rows instead of adopting the usual pseudo-
realism, but he gives their dance a sense of fun that makes
it seem entirely appropriate. Even when the children have
to be shown as becoming naughty and boisterous, their actions are carefully choreographed to the music. One stands
up and makes a rude gesture, another rises to take a swipe
at him and so on—all amusingly repeated exactly on the repeat of the tune. Throughout, Nureyev tells the story as far
as possible in dance rather than traditional mime.

The three duets for Clara with her dream prince, Drosselmeyer's alter ego, become the key sequences. The first, early in her dream, shows her still as a little girl and is composed with the couple dancing mainly side by side, drifting
romantically but chastely like the snowflakes that are
about to fill the stage. The few lifts are low and gentle. In
the second, Clara has begun her journey into a land of adventure; she is now lifted exultantly by her prince and her-

self moves in big arcs in his arms, but still there is some reticence. Finally, she sees herself as an adult. She changes from her simple dress into a glittering tutu and puts on an elaborate headdress before dancing this duet where she entrusts herself entirely to her prince's arms, ending triumphantly aloft. This last duet, interestingly, is based on one theme, that of the arabesque, presented throughout the dance in many variants from the opening pose, side by side but holding hands, to the final moment when the prince stands on one leg while holding her aloft.

Stylistically, emotionally and formally, these three duets mark a satisfying progression. More than any other *Nutcracker* I have ever seen, Nureyev's shows choreographically the child's growth toward accepting the idea that she must grow up. He has not made a children's ballet, as is so often the aim with this work (although children do enjoy his production), but has retrieved, possibly for the first time, the ballet's original concept as an adult entertainment. In the process he has abandoned the last remaining vestiges of the original nineteenth-century choreography. Some of these had remained until recent years in various productions, but it has to be admitted that either they had become gravely eroded by time or they cannot have been very interesting in the first place: probably, I would guess, a bit of each. By general consent, Ivanov's dances for the Snowflakes in 1892 were a remarkable advance in the art of choreography, introducing a symphonic style which has survived in the dances he created two years later for Act 2 of *Swan Lake*. But what was revolutionary then might look much less inspired if we could see it today exactly as it was then. I doubt, for instance, whether we would take happily to the idea of having the dancers wear headpieces from which sprouted wires covered with little white spheres (more like snowballs than snowflakes) and carry wands similarly ornamented, all these white blobs quivering at every step. In any case, Ivanov's elaborate star-shaped or circular patterns, for an ensemble of sixty dancers with eight soloists, seem to have been completely lost long ago. What Nureyev has invented for this music, complex patterns reflecting the crystalline shapes of snowflakes, is more beautiful than any version I have seen since Ashton's and admirably matched to the structure as well as the feeling of the music. I think it is not going too far to say that in this dance Nureyev, by an effort of imagination, has created a twentieth-century equivalent of the long-lost symphonic dance originally invented by Ivanov.

The only fragments of Ivanov's *Nutcracker* choreography which have survived in something close to their original form and are still worth preserving are his final pas de deux and the solo for the Sugar Plum Fairy. These, I am sure, will continue to be danced as a separate showpiece number and to be included in some productions of the full ballet. But it would have been silly for Nureyev to include them in his version, since the voluptuousness of the duet and the sharpness of the solo would both have clashed with his interpretation of the plot. Whereas in his *Raymonda* and *Sleeping Beauty* Nureyev takes dances from Petipa's productions as his starting point, there was no possibility of his doing the equivalent in *The Nutcracker.*

Another point about his *Nutcracker,* which explains much of its success, is the way he has managed, without detracting from the serious development of the theme or the splendor of its setting, to find an extraordinary amount of humor in the ballet. It warms his own incarnation as a gruff, kindly Drosselmeyer and inspires the grotesque dance for the deaf old grandfather. It is seen also in the disguises worn by Clara, her brother and her sister at the party, and the comic dances they perform while dressed up, also in several dances in the last act. The jokes are sharp but not cruel, and because the fun comes largely from eccentric movement, it remains funny even when seen many times.

Just one solo in this *Nutcracker* is taken unchanged from an earlier production. Nureyev obviously decided he could not improve upon the fast, twisting solo Vainonen had made for the Prince in Act 2, and he incorporated it with due acknowledgment. The rest is his own invention and maintains a high but not entirely uniform level of achievement. He has not yet, for instance, found a completely satisfactory way to present the scene where the dream turns momentarily to nightmare and Clara sees her family as a frightening group of bats. That is almost certainly because Tchaikovsky's music at that point, written to convey quite another idea, resists conversion. Elsewhere, when the invention is below his best, it is not for lack of ideas, but because he overgenerously tries to cram in so much. He is like a host who wants to offer his guests a buffet spread with an immense variety of delicacies. In private life such munificence is heartwarming, but the guests can pick and choose which they will take. In the theater the choice has to be made in advance by the producer. Some of Nureyev's choreography is so rich that it becomes a little indigestible. Happily, it is easier to discipline a too liberal prodigality of spirit than it is to reform niggardly meagerness, so with time the faults of his choreography should be overcome while its greater virtues remain, even enhanced.

There could hardly have been a greater contrast between the problems of rehabilitating *The Nutcracker* and those of preparing Nureyev's other outstanding Tchaikovsky production, *The Sleeping Beauty*. For this, he could keep closely

to the original plot and include much of the traditional choreography. For instance, the solos for the fairies in the prologue are among Petipa's finest inventions. The changes Nureyev has made to these may be decribed as editing or reorchestrating rather than rewriting. The first is cleaned up
slightly in its details to make it look more elegant than we
have usually seen of late. The second, perhaps to compen-
sate for being short, is shared by two girls dancing together,
sometimes in unison, sometimes in canon. The third is tak-
en rather faster than usual, the fourth somewhat slower; in
each case the change suits both music and choreography.

This sequence (there are six dances in all) is set in a new
frame which shows it off handsomely. The fairies enter,
with cavaliers and attendants, group by group from the
arches on one side of the stage, gradually filling the space
with a great swirling mass of movement in a good pastiche
of Petipa's style. At the end they have another ensemble in
which some old dance patterns are mingled with the new,
carefully designed to match. When the wicked fairy arrives,
her attendants seize the good fairies and sweep them
around the stage in a wild circle, a malevolent parody of
their first entry.

Where Nureyev's prologue differs radically from most
modern productions is in making the Lilac Fairy a nondanc-
ing role (this is actually a reversion to Petipa's original
treatment) and confronting her with a wicked fairy, Carabosse, who is a handsome woman instead of the usual hag,
although made sinister by the black snaky hair braided
around her head. The characters become more equally
matched adversaries, and the fairy tale shows more clearly
its intended meaning as a struggle between the forces of
darkness and light. That theme is stated metaphorically in
the ballet's opening moments, when courtiers descend an

enormous curved staircase bearing giant candelabra which convert darkness to light as they approach. Nureyev's designer for *The Sleeping Beauty* (as for the Vienna *Swan Lake, The Nutcracker,* except in Stockholm, and the latest *Raymonda*) is Nicholas Georgiadis. Their conception of the ballet is at first startlingly somber. Most of the dresses are in dark colors, and the settings are vast, overpowering, even somewhat gloomy. Only Aurora at first brings a touch of lighter color (and what could be more appropriate?), then Florimund when he appears with his hunting party, a foppish young prince. With each scene the setting becomes less oppressive and less grandiose so that in the last act, where many of the costumes are white, the effect is festive, although still more serious than is usual for this ballet.

This heaviness is not an arbitrary whim of producer and designer. As well as accentuate the underlying theme of a struggle between dark and light, it brings out an aspect of the music which is often ignored. Tchaikovsky's score has a brilliance which is reflected in the glitter of the choreography, but it also has great depth. No other production of the ballet which I have seen brings out the music's seriousness so well as Nureyev's. (I ought to add that my description here is of the original Milan production. Many details were changed in the revivals for the Canadian National Ballet and Festival Ballet, but the general effect was similar, although inevitably less good on smaller stages.)

He does not proceed only in one mood. Having established a prevailing style, which is derived from a view of the work as a whole instead of simply tackling each section in turn, he can afford to introduce variety which enriches the rest. Thus, Florimund is seen initially as a frivolous character. The hunting scene where he first appears is staged in a stretch of formal woodland with a terrace behind. The courtiers arrive in big coaches; Florimund strolls on last, elegant in pale green with a huge plumed hat, which he throws aside to take part in an arrow-throwing contest and score an insolently easy victory. At once he plunges with high spirits into a lively, square-cut country dance. Next, he allows himself to be blindfolded for a game of blindman's buff: an act of royal condescension which is explained when he cheats by looking under the cloth, thus maneuvering himself into position to steal a kiss from one particularly beautiful court lady. He insists on taking her hand for a minuet, but his attention seems to embarrass her, and she makes an excuse to rejoin her former partner. That nettles the Prince, who takes revenge when she invites him to depart in her coach, by escorting her to the door, then quietly snubbing her and remaining behind.

This leaves him alone in a ruffled mood, but Nureyev uses a generally neglected piece from the score (the entr'acte, andante sostenuto, with violin solo) to show the Prince's gradual awakening to a different state. The peace of the evening, expressed in both the music and a scenic change to a more open and romantic vista, works on him to bring a quiet serenity, revealed in a long, fluent and expressive solo which leads naturally into the Lilac Fairy's appearance and the vision of Aurora.

These changes offer a more interesting and varied characterization, heightening the ballet's action. There are more basic changes in Nureyev's treatment of the wedding celebration in Act 3. One is the insertion of a sarabande for the older courtiers, led by the King and Queen themselves (who normally have nothing to do but walk around or sit looking noble). Coming immediately before the pas de deux of Aurora and Florimund, it symbolizes the old order which is being replaced by the new as light finally triumphs. Elsewhere in this act he introduces some subtle differences of interpretation, as in the dance for the two cats, which becomes more courtly, so that it is clearly meant to be not two real cats, as in Petipa's original fairy tale version, but two people imitating catlike behavior, which makes it funnier and more interesting.

Some of Nureyev's production touches in *The Sleeping Beauty* involve only tiny details but do much to make sense of character and situation. To take only one example: when Aurora pricks her finger on the bouquet, she is hurt and momentarily frightened, obviously having been warned of the spell cast on her as a child (Aurora is usually left in inexplicable ignorance of this, a shameful lack of care on her parents' part). Then she realizes that thorns can do her no harm and quickly recovers. To reassure everybody, she begins plucking flowers from the bouquet and offers them to her father, mother and suitors. In doing this, she uncovers the spindle hidden in the middle of the bunch, and now she is terrified because she realizes what has happened. That leads naturally into the dance of dizziness from which she collapses into her hundred years' sleep.

Many people in recent years have attempted new stagings of *The Sleeping Beauty*. All start with the advantage that the work has come down to us more nearly intact than any other nineteenth-century Russian classic, needing less in the way of restoration or reinterpretation. The Prince's role seems meager in its original form, and some of the ensembles are not very practicable (Petipa used a large children's corps de ballet as well as adults). Ideally, my own inclination would be to keep as closely as possible to what remains of Petipa's original, making only such changes as are essential. But granted that you are going to depart from Petipa at all, which nowadays almost all producers do, nobody else has succeeded so well as Nureyev in keeping Petipa's spirit and structure. Others have, in fact, made fewer changes but, because these changes were less well judged, have ended up further from a satisfactory solution. Also, as I have already mentioned, Nureyev seems to me to do more justice than any rival to Tchaikovsky's music. It is a pity that for many years his production could be seen in only one European city, Milan, where it had infrequent performances, although it has been seen widely in North America since he revived it in 1972 for the National Ballet of Canada. The new production for Festival Ballet in 1975 was also planned to be suitable for touring.

The best of his other big-scale productions, *Don Quixote*, has happily been much more widely shown. Again, the European productions have been for comparatively minor companies, in Vienna and Marseilles, but his staging for the Australian Ballet has been shown on their tours of Europe and North America as well as at home and has also been brought to large audiences on film.

It is easy for people who do not really enjoy ballet to find fault with *Don Quixote*. If you want a logical story which could be told just as well in some other medium, you will probably be upset by the fact that the ballet owes little to Cervantes except its title, two characters and a few peripheral incidents. If you try to judge the music by the standards you would apply to a concert piece, Minkus' score may well seem tawdry. But the music was no more intended to be played without the dances than Verdi's opera accompaniments were meant to played without anyone singing, and Minkus' melodies are as marvelously shaped to inspire dancers as Verdi's for singers. And the plot was never designed to be more than an excuse for dancing, which it provides to perfection.

Even in a creaking, dusty old production (and we have seen examples, notably from the Bolshoi), *Don Quixote* can be fun to watch if it has the right dancers. Nureyev, by amending the order of scenes, omitting or changing some episodes and inserting new dances for the corps de ballet as well as the principals, makes the most of the ballet's virtues and adroitly overcomes or conceals its potential weaknesses. He has polished a lightweight work into one of ballet's most entertaining comedies.

Although the biggest changes he has made affect his own role of Basilio, the work is never just a one-man show. His adventures with Kitri, the heroine, take them from the busy harbor square of Barcelona to the windy, moonlit plain of Monteil, to a crowded tavern and eventually to a happy ending at their own wedding celebration. At each stage of this journey there are opportunities for swirling, pounding ensembles of townsfolk, toreadors, gypsies, revelers or guests. A dream vision brings a classical divertissement of dryads, and there are richly comic small parts for Kitri's foppish suitor, Gamache, as well as Don Quixote and Sancho Panza. Also, as always, Nureyev made sure that the ballerina had a really rewarding role, polishing and supplementing what was already a glittering part for a dancer with personality, wit and virtuosity.

For his own role, surviving versions of the old ballet offered the basis of an amusing characterization, although with only one big display dance, in the famous pas de deux. It was a part he had already played with success in Russia, but he has built it up into something prodigious. It still looks good, even when other dancers take over the role in his absence, but nobody else brings quite the same sparkling audacity to it. He manages to be everywhere at once: flirting with Kitri and her friends, too, picking his prospective father-in-law's pocket to prove that he could support the old man's daughter, teasing Don Quixote, tossing Kitri nonchalantly high over his head when they dance together, bounding all over the stage in a series of joyously exuberant solos. It is a performance of tremendous zest, but also of perfect control. How is it, for example, that when he pretends to stab himself (thus tricking Kitri's father into a blessing over the "corpse" which can be interpreted as his long-withheld consent to the wedding), his collapse flat on his back always leaves the wide brim of his hat pointing absolutely straight up into the air? His timing in this sequence is extraordinary: interrupting his feigned death, whenever he judges that nobody is looking, to swallow a drink, steal a kiss or trip a passing ankle.

I am not sure what is the more impressive about his Basilio: the almost outrageously high, broad leaps, the breakneck circuits and pinpoint landings which characterize his solos or the tiny details of his acting. It is remarkable, in fact, to what an extent his acting is done through his dancing. As he grabs repeatedly at Kitri's foot, for instance, in one of their dances together, his different reaction at every attempt reveals the playful affection that underlies the shifting moods of their relationship.

It is almost tempting to look for an autobiographical element in his portrait of the young man who, with nothing but his native wit to help him, manages to end up a winner while others who started with every advantage come a cropper. Cheek, ingenuity and bravado are the means by which he romps to success. However, there is no need to look for hidden meanings in a work and a performance of such entertaining high spirits. If one did want to point a moral, it could equally well be the value in ballet of trusting the expressive power of dancing. Even the duel between

Don Quixote and Gamache, often treated as a slightly pointless incident, becomes in his hands a comic duet, almost formal in its patterns, and in the transformation from mime to dance it is made more relevant as well as funnier.

There is no doubt in my mind that the movie of *Don Quixote* which Nureyev conceived and codirected is by far the best of the films he has appeared in. His abilities are better documented on film than any other comparable dancer, starting with two early films in which he danced *The Corsair* pas de deux, one made in Russia, the other in Britain. The latter, *An Evening with the Royal Ballet,* also shows him in *Les Sylphides.* Feature-length films in which he has appeared since then are his Vienna *Swan Lake,* the Royal Ballet's *Romeo and Juliet* and the documentary *I Am a Dancer.* A somewhat cut version of his *Sleeping Beauty* was made for television, and of course, he has danced innumerable times in shorter pieces on television, some of these appearances recorded for posterity. In addition, a friend of his has privately filmed many of Nureyev's productions.

Nureyev would find fault with many, perhaps all of these, but they have ensured that his talents have been seen by many thousands, probably millions, of people who would never set foot inside a theater, also that future generations will not have to take reports of his prodigious skill on trust. The *Don Quixote* film does more than that. Besides recording a fine production and a superb performance, it reveals a startling ability in another medium. The adaptation of the stage version, the choice of angles and sequences, the way the cameras are used to reveal what is really important in any moment of the action, but without the jumpy nudging of the audience's attention that mars many ballet films—these qualities have eluded the great majority of professional filmmakers who tried to capture ballet on the screen. Nureyev beats them at their own game.

Given his nature and his past record, that is less surprising than would otherwise be the case. A gift for picking up essentials serves him in all aspects of his daily life, and he is anyway an assiduous moviegoer, seeing the same film several times if it appeals to him. He is not the sort to enjoy what he sees without thought; the same analysis and questioning he brings to ballet are at work all the time. Also, he has a flair for knowing what is good and bad even in a medium that is not familiar to him. Nigel Gosling told me of their collaboration in the English version of Nureyev's autobiography when he first came to Britain; at that time he spoke only a little English but was already able to pounce on anything that sounded not his style.

There are things in the *Don Quixote* film which Nureyev would do differently if he had the chance again. Some of the sound dubbing was done in his absence, not always as he would have wished. The quality of the color in the prints was a constant vexation to him. Also, the amazingly tight schedule for the whole enterprise made it impossible to go back over some scenes for a second time as he would have wished. But whatever reservations there might be about some details, the total effect is impressive, and he told me that he would like to have the chance to try filming his *Nutcracker* and *Sleeping Beauty* also in his own way, with strong companies.

That must raise the thought whether, when he eventually has to stop dancing, he might get sidetracked into a second career in films. The idea might sound farfetched, but it is a lot less preposterous than the likelihood of that untrained boy in far-off Ufa ever becoming the most famous male dancer in the world. On the other hand, having devoted his life to ballet so far, he seems to me more likely to continue in ballet. There are many obvious things he could do. He has already shown himself unusually gifted coaching dancers in their roles, and not only soloists, because when he works with a company on one of his own productions, you can see his impact right through to the most junior members of the corps de ballet. I have never seen this more vividly demonstrated than when I spent four consecutive nights in Milan, watching the local ballet company. Two of those performances were of his *Sleeping Beauty*, and on the other nights they danced the local repertory. Admittedly the *Beauty* performances had the presence of Fonteyn and Nureyev as a special stimulus for the dancers, but the immensely popular Italian ballerina Carla Fracci was appearing on the other nights, one of which included a new work specially created for her. Frankly, the dancers looked like a different company on the Nureyev nights: far more alert, exact, stylish and interesting.

Something of that sort happens whenever he works intensively with a company. How much more might he achieve as a permanent director, using his experience, knowledge, flair and intelligence to mold the repertory, influence the style, spot and develop potential talent, bring in new influences. The dancers would have to work hard because he is not a person to accept complacency or second best, but those who had talent and were prepared to make the most of themselves would almost certainly find themselves achieving more than they thought possible.

Nureyev has already turned down invitations to direct more than one company, primarily because of a wish to put his own dancing career first. Such invitations will undoubtedly be repeated in future, and the likeliest guess is that he will accept. I would like to think that it will be the Royal

Ballet, with which he has been so closely associated over the years, that has the imagination to secure his services in this different capacity, since no rival of comparable ability is to be seen, and whichever company wins him is sure to enjoy a degree of eminence.

He is a discerning and enthusiastic admirer of many talented choreographers and always ready for new experiences, so it is inconceivable that any company he ran would find itself narrowly circumscribed in its choice of new productions. But his own creative potential is such that its future development also arouses expectations of much interest. Having satisfied himself with *Tancredi* that he is able to do it, he is unlikely at this stage of his career to commit himself to the expenditure of time that would be needed to create further ballets from scratch. However, what he has done in the way of staging, refurbishing, supplementing or even completely reworking old ballets has already revealed a keen stagecraft, an exceptionally responsive ear for music and a command of the classical tradition that is unrivaled among his contemporaries.

All this leads me to believe that what Nureyev still has to offer may prove to be even more than he has achieved so far. He has left his mark indelibly on the history of ballet; he could go on to influence its future even more profoundly.

Meanwhile, what exactly has he achieved? He has made himself not only the dancer he wanted to be as a child, but an international star, whose name and face are known not just to ballet lovers, but to the general public. Like the few others who have achieved this sort of celebrity, he has thus helped make ballet more popular and attract new audiences. He has been an example, inspiration and practical help to a whole generation of dancers. He has brought pleasure to people all over the world who have seen and admired his artistry. He has helped to breathe new life into old ballets and to win opportunities and recognition for living choreographers whose work he thinks worth encouraging.

Yet I have a feeling that he would want to be judged on his achievements as a dancer, his actual performances onstage. One interesting point is that literally nobody can have seen the whole of his career, starting from his student days in the Soviet Union and traveling subsequently all around the world. I counted up the number of companies with which I have seen him dance—sixteen of them onstage and some more on film—but that is only a fraction of those with which he has appeared. Similarly, although I have seen him in nearly sixty roles, there are about another two dozen which I have missed, either because he has not danced them since he left the USSR, or because he gave them a few times only (sometimes just once) on his travels. However, I have seen him in almost every major role he has taken since coming to the West, and many of his minor or fugitive parts too.

Trying to choose which, among them all, I would rate as his outstanding performances, I find myself scribbling down one name after another. For most people, it is his interpretations of the full-evening classics which must come first. For well over a decade his Albrecht in *Giselle,* his Siegfried in *Swan Lake* and his Florimund in *The Sleeping Beauty* have illuminated these old ballets. I have watched him dance all of them many times in different productions, and in all those years I have never seen a dull performance from him. His standard has varied, when he was going through one of the difficult patches that occur in any dancer's career, when he was overtired or had been concentrating on new roles in different styles. But even Nureyev's off nights have him dancing with more strength and panache than most dancers can produce at their best.

He has the gift, too, to make these conventional heroes come alive, to make you see in a new light gestures you have taken for granted, to be surprised even by a ballet you know well. His feeling for style is impeccable, his response to familiar music always fresh. Also, not only is it his own performance that is so good, but his alertness has its effect on everyone around him. This is apparent whoever he dances with, but the more able his partner, the better the result. With Fonteyn especially the relationship has always been close and subtle. It was a drama critic, Charles Lewsen of the *Times*, who told me that he had seen this pair only once, and what impressed him above all was the way their eyes seemed hardly ever to leave each other, maintaining a contact which ran between them like an electric current. I supposed that it must been a modern, dramatic work in which he saw them, but no, it was *Swan Lake*. My colleague was struck, too, by the fact that they preserved a style of high romantic acting which has completely vanished from the straight dramatic stage.

The opportunity to dance, at the beginning of his career, with such ballerinas as Dudinskaya and Shelest at the Kirov, then so often with Fonteyn and sometimes with other distinguished Western ballerinas, was an immense asset to Nureyev, giving him an example of artistry to spur his own performances to their highest potential, but over the years he has repaid that debt. With Fonteyn, the influence worked both ways. Her experience, poise and quietness drew more depth from him; his understanding of technique and the fire of his personality enabled her to reveal a passion that had previously been overlaid by other considerations.

Now that he often dances with ballerinas less experienced than himself, that spur is no longer available to Nureyev, but although an unresponsive partner can detract from his performance, he seems to find inspiration in helping others develop their potential, not by encouraging them to imitate their seniors, but in the way their own best qualities suggest. It could be easy for Nureyev to concentrate on his own dancing and let others look after themselves, but that is not his nature; he wants everything right because otherwise he cannot be at his best.

Bruhn's influence as well as Fonteyn's can be seen in the way Nureyev's performances in the classics have developed. The two men paced each other as champion runners do: both had proved how much they could achieve even before they met, but went on to greater achievements thanks to a relationship combining competition and friendly rivalry. It would be pleasant if over the next few years we might see a similar result from the arrival in the West of Mikhail Baryshnikov, another favorite pupil of Nureyev's old teacher Pushkin, who left the Kirov for greater artistic opportunities. This time Nureyev is the more developed artist, the other the newcomer full of youthful freshness, but their relationship could be as fruitful, although it does not necessarily follow that the two men would find the same close rapport and understanding offstage as on. I have quoted Bruhn's description of how Nureyev and he worked together. The effect of that can be seen in the way Nureyev pared all inessentials away from his characterizations and concentrated on bringing out the essence of each role. I would say, too, that the sharp clarity which Nureyev nowadays brings to his classical dancing derives from Bruhn's example; it heightens the impact of the pace and punch and fluency which he always had.

Bruhn also helped Nureyev widen his range by introducing him to the Danish classics as a supplement to the Russian tradition. Nureyev's interpretation of James in *La Sylphide* is one of the finest things I have ever seen him do. In Copenhagen, where the ballet originated, I have heard it suggested that although his dancing of the role is marvelous, it is outside the proper style, but Bruhn told me that people made exactly the same objection to him when he first took the role, only later deciding that he was their best protagonist. What Nureyev certainly has in the role is the quality its choreographer, Bournonville, most valued in his own dancing, "a kind of manly joie de vivre." Where he differs markedly from most Danish dancers is in the heavy emphasis he puts on some steps, compared with their nimble lightness. You can see this especially in the Scottish reel where he gets nearer, perhaps, to a genuine folk dance style than the stylized version of it. But his downthrust brings out more strongly, by contrast, the incisive flight of his movements in the classical solos, the immensely powerful thrust into the air for the steps of virtuosity which he displays so clearly. Also, his eagerness brings the character to life as someone who really could go chasing after an ideal.

No need, at this stage, to say more about his other classical roles in his own productions, except as a reminder of the way these have enabled him to maintain a wider repertory than the international guest circuit would otherwise make possible. Also it is worth noting that in some of these, such as *La Bayadère* and *The Corsair* pas de deux, we can see something of the bold, heroic style which Nureyev would have been required to concentrate on had he remained in Russia. There, even in the most favorable circumstances possible, he would have lacked most of the influences he found in the West. Some aspects of his dancing he would have developed to a greater degree; it is easy to imagine what a performance he might have given in, say, a ballet like *Spartacus,* and doubtless he would have developed his own choreographic gifts there as here. But many aspects of his dancing would have remained dormant, both through the stylistic restrictions of modern Russian ballet, which has concentrated superbly on a grand sweep but generally at the expense of detail, and through the social requirement to produce art with a positive message. It must be a matter for regret that the Soviet Union, which could offer Nureyev a schooling better than he could get anywhere else in the world, could not make use of his artistry once it had developed and that the barriers to free communication prevented the Russians from ever seeing what use he had made of the gifts they helped nurture.

In the Soviet Union, he would doubtless in time have danced *Les Sylphides,* having already performed the duet from it, but it was actually in the West that he took this and several other roles from the surviving repertory of the Diaghilev Ballet (another exile whose work was never properly seen in his homeland). Nureyev's solo in *Les Sylphides* quite simply has no equal among contemporary dancers; even the best rivals lack that apparently unforced strength and accuracy, that way of floating on the music. Another ballet by the same choreographer, Fokine, provided him with an interesting role once he had overcome a false start in it. His Petrushka nowadays makes very poignant the theme of a doll endowed with a living spirit; one notable factor when I saw him dance it in Paris was that he wore a much lighter makeup than is customary, so that his own face, visible through the doll-like painted features, became an image of the spirit struggling to reveal itself. It is vexing to think how near he came to dancing Fokine's *Spectre de*

212

la rose when he first came West: perhaps he might have given some idea of what Nijinsky was like in it, because in those days Tamara Karsavina, who danced *Spectre* with Nijinsky, remarked on the resemblance. But it is a young man's role, and he is never likely to do it now.

I would like to see Nureyev dance another Nijinsky role, the only one surviving with Nijinsky's own choreography, *L'Après-midi d'un faune.* Robbins' modern-dress *Afternoon of a Faun,* to the same Debussy music, is to some extent a commentary on Nijinsky's treatment of antique myth, and when Nureyev first danced Robbins' ballet, a fierce quality, like an animal, showed through the smooth surface. He has refined that away, and now dances Robbins' ballet with the ambiguously understated delicacy it needs, leaving the audience to decide whether or not there was a real emotion passing between the boy and girl who practice together one hot afternoon in a ballet studio. But it would be fascinating to see him also in the more intense atmosphere of the earlier ballet. I have already discussed *Dances at a Gathering,* another of Robbins' works which provides Nureyev with one of his most rewarding parts. Nothing has come so far of Robbins' thought of creating a role for Nureyev in a new work, but one may hope for the future.

A choreographer who has made several roles for Nureyev is Kenneth MacMillan. Romeo is one he particularly enjoys dancing, and it enables him to deploy a wide range of emotion. From a purely dancing point of view, his solos and duets with Juliet in the garden scene beneath her balcony are the highlight of his performance, his body apparently whipped into movement by the intensity of his new feelings. But other moments are memorable: the byplay with Mercutio and Benvolio, full of good-humored comradeship; the capricious way he interrupts Juliet's friends when they are dancing at the ball; the teasing of the nurse when she brings Juliet's letter; then the way he jumps around the stage for joy after reading it and plants a kiss on the messenger's surprised lips before rushing off to the church to marry. Some of his other MacMillan roles (in *Images of Love, Divertimento* and *Manon*) have been discussed earlier. The spoof circus duet *Sideshow,* which MacMillan made for Nureyev and Seymour, was disappointingly slight, but it did show off some startling technical feats, such as Nureyev's spinning through the air with his arm tight behind his back.

For sheer uninhibited display of emotion, it would be difficult to beat Nureyev's performance in Maurice Béjart's *Rite of Spring,* full of despair at knowing himself picked out for sacrifice. The *Lieder eines fahrenden Gesellen* which Béjart specially created for Nureyev also allowed him to play with immense skill on the emotions of his audience, and although the role itself was rather abstract, Nureyev gave the dances an incisively tragic character.

There is, of course, no characterization at all in Paul Taylor's *Aureole,* the lyrical suite of dances to Handel music which provides one of Nureyev's favorite modern dance roles, but the choreography presents such an original style that it has a flavor all its own and must be very satisfying to dance. For Nureyev, an additional attraction of the part is that it is so far removed from his usual classical style. The ballet is "classical" in the other sense of the word—in its serene use of form to create a sense of the joyous tranquillity—but the dances are far removed from ballet technique. They involve long static poses, sudden bursts of wild energy, slow fluid stretchings, a contrast between explosive leaps and falls. When Taylor himself dances it, the movement has an extraordinary smoothness, and part of the interest of watching Nureyev in it, for anyone who knows his work well, comes from the effort he has to make to adapt himself to it. The role depends on looking relaxed, but for him that relaxation is itself, paradoxically, a strain. That he can dance it at all is a tribute to his willpower and adaptability; that he can make it look so authentic is a triumph of his spirit.

The other ballet Nureyev has danced with Taylor's company is *The Book of Beasts,* where his role is a series of comic interventions in the form of various mythical creatures. In the finale Taylor included an episode parodying a ballet sequence, which was very funny when he danced the role himself. Taylor told me that he would have been happy, when Nureyev played the role, for him to adapt this to his own gifts, but it is interesting that Nureyev was so eager to dance the work as set, that in fact, what he did at that point was a comic imitation of a modern dancer imitating a classical dancer.

To say that modern dance and classical ballet present an antithesis is true, but only part of the truth. Just as there is a world of difference between the work of various ballet choreographers, so there is between different modern dance creators. José Limón in *The Moor's Pavane* is working at the opposite end of the spectrum from *Aureole;* although he too uses old music (in this case, Purcell) and sets the dances in formal style, they are used to convey the essence of Othello's tragedy, part of the effect coming from the way emotion struggles through the formal restraints of the dances and eventually shatters them. Nureyev does not make up as a black man for this role: a slight darkening of his features is enough for an exotic appearance (which was true also of Limón himself, a Mexican). It is not the tragedy of a black man, but of any jealous man, that he is convey-

215

ing, and he brings an overwhelming wounded strength to the tragic ending.

It was with Rudi van Dantzig that Nureyev began his exploration of the modern idiom. Whereas Taylor and Limón both made their careers entirely in the modern style, Van Dantzig's initial training has been in classic ballet, although he was influenced by the most famous of contemporary modern dancers, Martha Graham, when he started creating ballets. In *Monument for a Dead Boy*, he worked in an incisive way, making short scenes representing different aspects of the hero's life: from impressionist drama, such as the squalid lovemaking of his parents, who are shown as heavy, lumpish people, far removed from the usual ballet character, to a scene where the hero is sexually assaulted by a group of school friends, through to lyrical episodes with a young girl. The central figure has to bind the various episodes together, giving purpose and point to each, but consequently does not himself play a very positive role. Nureyev learned something from dancing the part, but no wonder he asked Van Dantzig for a less passive role when *The Ropes of Time* was created for him.

The fact that the central figure in *Ropes* is called the Traveler emphasizes a generic likeness with other roles Nureyev had to play (Petit's *L'Estasi* and Béjart's Mahler ballet are notable examples) in which he represented a man journeying through life and suffering on the way. There seemed a danger that like Humphrey Bogart, Nureyev would find himself playing the same role over and over: playing it better than anyone else could, but revealing only a fragment of himself in the process. Happily, Nureyev avoided that trap. *Ropes* actually offered far more variety than a brief summary of its theme would suggest. The duets with the two women were strongly contrasted, and a group of young men, coming on fresh and dancing in direct competition with the star who had already been at full stretch for some time, provided a startling dramatic and choreographic challenge. Also, the large abstract sculptures of Van Schayk's decor, themselves moving about the stage, showed off the protagonist in rapidly varying circumstances.

The other modern dance choreographer with whom Nureyev has worked closely is Glen Tetley. As previously mentioned, Tetley trained in both ballet and modern dance, but has sometimes shown a tendency to push dancers toward whatever is least familiar to them. When he worked with the Royal Ballet, his styles emphasized its modern extreme, although in *Field Figures* the heavy, rather static role which Nureyev danced was contrasted with a quick, light, more brilliant part for the second man. In *Laborintus* the epic scope of the Berio score and the importance of the sung or spoken text forced the ballet into the shape of a myth where there was little difference in the degree of prominence given to the characters.

It was in *Tristan* that the choreographic relationship of Tetley and Nureyev came to its height. With a score lasting about three-quarters of an hour, offering great contrasts of every sort (tone, volume, style, material, sonority, mood) the scope for a heroic creation was present. Again, Tetley gave the most obviously effective solos to the supporting characters, and the way Nureyev remained the center of attention in spite of this is remarkable. His role was built largely on difficult balances, long-held poses, slow sinking, in all of which he showed exceptional strength and control. Also he gave the gestures a vivid expressiveness. I can imagine no other dancer who could carry off the part, but it had two elements holding it back from being the great created role which Nureyev and his audiences must eagerly hope for every time he undertakes something new. One was the fact that it made no revelation of something unexpected in the dancer. By concentrating on one aspect of his talent and stretching it in a special way, it made him look different, but what he did had already been present, latent or active, in other performances. The other limitation came from the dramatic structure of the work, or rather the fact that Tetley avoided a dramatic structure at all, simply reflecting themes and episodes from the story of Tristan and Isolde in contemplative mood. That is enormously difficult to do on such a big scale and, for all the skill of the choreographer and dancers, could not hold the audience's undivided interest.

The importance of *Tristan* lay in giving him at last a modern dance role that is uniquely his, even if a flawed one. *The Ropes of Time* has been given without him (Van Schayk danced the lead in a revival for the Dutch National Ballet), and *Laborintus,* being essentially a team work, has been done by other casts. All of Nureyev's other modern dance roles were created for other people, and although Nureyev does them well, he could hardly be expected to be better than Taylor himself in *Aureole* or Limón in *The Moor's Pavane.* Even *Tristan* has in fact been danced by someone else, but only when Nureyev was unavailable for one of a run of performances; the work was built so much around his muscles that it is difficult to imagine what it would look like without him.

Is it true, then, as some people have suggested, that he would be better to leave such roles to others who concentrate entirely on them and himself to spend his time doing what he does uniquely well? With most dancers, the answer would have to be yes, but I feel it would not be in Nureyev's nature to leave a whole area of experience untasted. He has a compulsion to try everything. True, spending time on a different technique, forcing his muscles into unfamiliar ways, does sometimes affect his classical dancing, but it has never been only for a fine technique that he stands out, rather for the expressive use of that technique. His interest in new experience, his wish for different ways of using movement are part of him and help make his performances in classical roles the joy they are.

Yet it is what he can do with classical ballet which shows him at his greatest, and not only in the old classics. Among living choreographers the two whose works have evoked his best performances are the two masters of the academic tradition, Ashton and Balanchine. He has danced only four Balanchine ballets, and one of those only a few times, early in his career. But the other three show three different sides of his work, all of them excellent. In *Agon* it is nothing but sheer muscular dance: tough, fast, powerful. In *The Prodigal Son,* the dance is used for an expressionist version of the parable, twisted to a different significance from the Bible story. (There is no fatted calf, no jealous brother, only repentance and forgiveness in the homecoming.) Biblical the work may be, but not solemn: a surplus of energy and adventurousness is shown as the motive for leaving on his travels, symbolized in quick, impatient bursts of movement. Comedy and sexiness mark the middle scenes: stamping drunkenly with the drinking companions, ritually seduced by the siren in dance images of explicit exactness; finally, dragging himself away from the scene of his disgrace, completely shamed, and crawling home on his knees, filthy and in rags. In *Apollo,* the movement is less explicit: when danced by other people, the ballet can look almost plotless, simply a divertissement. But there is an underlying story of the god's birth, his growing up, his games with the muses, whose first efforts at art he judges, and finally the realization of the divinity within him, whereupon he climbs the steps toward heaven. More than anyone else I have ever seen in the role, Nureyev makes that content clear when he dances, but he is also outstanding for the way he actually dances the steps, the sharp cutting edge he gives the dances, thanks to the exactness and strength of his dancing. To see such excellence of pure dance irradiated by such humanity is a rare pleasure, and when he has to suggest the godhead within, swooning onto the muses' arms at the realization of it, then drawing himself up for a slow progress around the stage, there genuinely is a transfiguration that is most moving. If I could only ever see Nureyev again in one role, I should be tempted to make that role Apollo.

But the old classics would provide keen opposition, and so would the ballets of Frederick Ashton. Armand, of course, where he achieves such nuances of confidence and despair, love and bitterness and where Ashton has achieved one uniquely thrilling moment of absolute simplicity. While Marguerite is dying, the music begins to sound Armand's agitated approach, and then suddenly, behind the open framework of Cecil Beaton's setting, he can be seen running in a great arc across the back of the stage, his cloak flowing behind him, only to disappear into the wings and then at the last moment to arrive again at the front of the stage, hurling the cloak from him and rushing to take the dying Marguerite in his arms. Nothing but running across a stage, but what he makes of it!

At the opposite extreme Ashton made Friday's Child in *Jazz Calendar* for Nureyev, and nobody else has quite caught the sinuously smoochy blues quality of the dance, the mixture of playfulness and mockery and sincerity. Among his other Ashton roles, I look forward to another chance to see his Oberon and the chance also to see what he could make of the whole of *Apparitions*. And of course, there is his latest Ashton role, Colas. He was offered the part when he first began to dance with the Royal Ballet but put it off because he was planning to revive *The Corsair* pas de deux and did not want to spoil the impact of his similar solo in that. Then nobody repeated the offer until recently, when he accepted with obvious delight. Actually, I wonder whether the young Nureyev would have been as good in *La Fille mal gardée* as he is now. Memory is deceptive; we think of Nureyev at the beginning of the 1960s as having had very long hair, but pictures prove that he did not then wear it so long as he does now. It is just that he started wearing it longer while almost everyone else had it very short, so it looked startling at the time. (The same is true of the Beatles: how neat and scrubbed those early pictures look now, which caused such excitement at the time.) If one misremembers a simple fact like length of hair, how definite can we be about other matters? But I have a conviction, which I think few would dispute, that young Nureyev was a dancer whose intense romanticism might have been out of place in Ashton's simple pastoral comedy. His dancing over the years has grown sharper, but he has mellowed, to the point where the quiet humor of *Fille* shows him uniquely relaxed and full of charm. Perhaps, in a way, Ashton was the choreographer destined to surprise Nureyev, not by finding something new in him, but by making him reveal onstage something of the warmth, humor and sympathy which he shows in private life.

No one role, however, is by any stretch of imagination going to reveal the whole of him. Remember how the Rus-

221

sians, before he left the Kirov, compared him to Chabukiani, a dancer of fiery heroism. Then, when he reached London, people who knew Nijinsky well, that creature of ambiguous magic, thought Nureyev was like him. How can
one person possibly resemble two others, so different, almost at opposite poles? Only by containing within himself
contradictions and multiple facets. Perhaps that is part of
his secret.

There is a question I have left unasked until now, but it
has to be faced before I end. Is he the greatest male dancer in
the world? In a way, the question is meaningless. If I think
of the finest male dancers I have ever seen, I find that every
one is in some way unique. Jean Babilée had a theatricality
nobody else equaled, Igor Youskevitch a kind of majesty,
André Eglevsky a divine simplicity. Who can match the eccentric comedy of Alexander Grant, the heroic fervor of
Vladimir Vassiliev, the *joie de vivre* of Edward Villella?
Erik Bruhn's nobility and dramatic clarity are unmatched;
Mikhail Baryshnikov has a deep sense of involvement and a
keen sense of style. Can any man except Jaap Flier move me
to tears with his dancing, or anyone else convey the feeling
of sheer goodness that Paul Taylor does? What about Merce
Cunningham, whose quality lies in the authority and integ-
rity of his movement? The list could be extended, but you
see the point already. To say that one of them is unambiguously greater than others involves first a choice of what
constitutes greatness.

With ballerinas it is easier to be dogmatic. I know without hesitation that Galina Ulanova is the greatest ballerina
I have ever seen and that after her Margot Fonteyn stands
far above any rival. But does that mean that Ulanova and
Fonteyn are both incomparably above any male dancer
since they stand out so much more unambiguously than

222

any man does? Or is it that among men the competition is more fierce?

Whatever the reason, there are certain qualities shared by Ulanova and Fonteyn which perhaps help define those aspects of a dancer's work which tend to true greatness. There is a directness of communication in both of them, which can extend to any member of the audience however much or little that person knows about the art of dancing. There is a humanity which illuminates their roles and an absorption which makes them seem, while dancing, actually to embody the character they are playing rather than just represent it.

Illumination: the act of lighting up, from within, the action or character being shown. Perhaps that, above all, is the criterion. But then one must make a distinction in respect of both the extent and the brightness of the light thrown. One dancer may shine brightly within a limited field. Another brings the brightness of day to a much larger area. Is there any doubt where greatness lies?

Nureyev himself never doubted that Erik Bruhn was the greatest male dancer of the day, and instinct and reason combine to make me agree. Tragedy and comedy, old works and new, great ballets and tawdry ones, he danced them all with insight, nobility, humility and a relentless determination that each performance should be better than the one before.

But Bruhn had to give up dancing because his body could no longer endure the strain his perfectionism put upon it, and although he has returned to the stage, it is only within a more limited range of roles. One person remains whom Bruhn could regard as working in the same way, "always trying for something more." He too has the range, the expressiveness, the power to illuminate.

223

I do not think it really matters too much how one places names in an order of merit. The enjoyment of excellence, large or small, wherever it can be found, is more rewarding. Many dancers may achieve, in their own way, their own greatness. But if Rudolf Nureyev is not the greatest of them today, who is?

Nureyev's Roles

ARRANGED as far as possible in chronological order of his first appearance in each. For those he took before leaving the Soviet Union, the attribution of roles to seasons has had to be reconstructed from memory and is therefore only approximate. The older classics which he has danced with many companies vary to some extent from one production to another; to record every minor change would be both impracticable and pointless, but substantially different versions of the same ballet are included as separate entries.

Ballet and role	Choreographer and composer	Notes
1955–57		
All in student performances at the Leningrad Ballet School		
Solo from DIANA AND ACTEON	Vakhtang Chabukiani Cesare Pugni	See also under 1957–58

*Indicates that he danced the premiere of the new work or new choreography.
†Indicates that he danced the premiere of the new production or revival of an existing work.

Ballet and role	Choreographer and composer	Notes
Vaczlav's solo from THE FOUNTAIN OF BAKHCHISARAI	Rostislav Zakharov Boris Asafiev	
Pas de deux from GISELLE, Act 2	Marius Petipa, after Jean Coralli and Jules Perrot Adolphe Adam	See also under 1959–60
PAS DE QUATRE	Alexander Pushkin ? music	
Pas de deux from CHOPINIANA (Les Sylphides)	Mikhail Fokine Frédéric Chopin	See also under 1961–62

1957–58

THE NUTCRACKER The Prince	Vassili Vainonen Piotr Tchaikovsky	First in public performances with the Kirov Ballet while still a student; kept role on joining the company. See also under 1961–62 and 1967–68
SWAN LAKE Pas de trois	Marius Petipa Tchaikovsky	In public performances with the Kirov Ballet while still a student
Pas de deux from SWAN LAKE, Act 2	Lev Ivanov Tchaikovsky	In student performances. See also under 1960–61

NUREYEV'S ROLES

Ballet and role	Choreographer and composer	Notes
Pas de deux from SWAN LAKE , Act 3	Petipa Tchaikovsky	In student performances. See also under 1960–61
DIANA AND ACTEON Pas de deux from the ballet ESMERALDA	Perrot, reproduced by Agrippina Vaganova; Acteon's solo by Chabukiani Pugni	In Moscow competition. Later revived and occasionally danced this in the West
Scene from GAYANE (Kurdish dance)	Nina Anisimova Aram Khachaturian	In Moscow competition. See also under 1959–60
Pas de deux from THE CORSAIR	After Petipa; man's solo by Chabukiani Riccardo Drigo and Ludwig Minkus	In Moscow competition. In his repertory ever since with many companies
Solo from LAURENCIA	Chabukiani Alexander Krein	In student performances. See also under 1958–59

1958

All with Kirov Ballet

LAURENCIA Frondoso	Chabukiani Krein	See also under 1963–64
*VALSE VOLONTÉ	Leonid Yakobson ? music	

Ballet and role	Choreographer and composer	Notes
THE RED POPPY Pas de quatre 1959–60	Alexei Andreyev Reinhold Gliere	

All with Kirov Ballet

DON QUIXOTE Basilio	After Petipa and Alexander Gorsky Minkus and others	See also under 1966–67
GISELLE Albrecht	Petipa, after Coralli and Perrot Adam	In his repertory ever since with many companies
LA BAYADÈRE Solor	Petipa, revised by Chabukiani Minkus	Danced the full ballet only in Leningrad, but see also under 1963–64
THE SLEEPING BEAUTY Bluebird	Petipa Tchaikovsky	Also danced this later with Cuevas Ballet and on one U.S. tour with Royal Ballet
RAYMONDA Pas de quatre	Petipa Alexander Glazunov	See also under 1961–62 and 1963–64
GAYANE Armen	Anisimova Khachaturian	Later revived and occasionally danced a pas de deux from this
MOSZKOVSKY WALTZ	Vainonen Moritz Moszkovsky	

1960–61

All with Kirov Ballet

NUREYEV'S ROLES

Ballet and role	Choreographer and composer	Notes
Pas de deux from THE FLAMES OF PARIS	Vainonen Asafiev	
*WALTZ	Yakobson Richard Strauss (from DER ROSENKAVALIER)	
LEGEND OF LOVE Ferhad	Yuri Grigorovich Arif Melikov	Danced a dress rehearsal but not a public performance
SWAN LAKE Prince Siegfried	Petipa and Ivanov Tchaikovsky	In his repertory ever since with many companies; see also under 1961–62, 1963–64, 1964–65, 1969–70 and 1972–73
THE SLEEPING BEAUTY Prince Désiré (also called Florimund)	Petipa, revised by Konstantin Sergeyev Tchaikovsky	In his repertory ever since with several companies. See also under 1966–67 and 1968–69
Cossack camp scene from TARAS BULBA Andrei	Boris Fenster Vassili Soloviev-Sedoy	
1961–62		
†LE SPECTRE DE LA ROSE The Spirit	Nureyev, after Fokine Carl Maria von Weber	For TV program in Frankfurt; has not danced the role since
*POÈME TRAGIQUE	Frederick Ashton Alexander Scriabin	For his London debut at RAD gala; danced on this occasion only

Ballet and role	Choreographer and composer	Notes
LA FILLE MAL GARDÉE Colas	Joseph Lazzini Peter Ludwig Hertel	With the Marseilles Ballet, this season only. See also under 1962–63 and 1973–74
*TOCCATA AND FUGUE	Erik Bruhn Johann Sebastian Bach	In concert performances with Sonia Arova, Rosella Hightower and Erik Bruhn in Cannes and Paris. For *Raymonda*, see also under 1963–64
*DANCES FROM RAYMONDA	Nureyev, after Petipa Glazunov	
*FANTAISIE	Bruhn Alonso y Belda, Soutillo y Vert, Guerrero	
*Pas de deux from THE NUTCRACKER	Nureyev, after Vainonen Tchaikovsky	With Hightower for their concert group. See also under 1967–68
Pas de deux from FLOWER FESTIVAL AT GENZANO	August Bournonville, revised by Bruhn Edvard Helsted and Holger Simon Paulli	First with Arova for their concert group; in his repertory ever since with several companies
LES SYLPHIDES	Fokine Chopin	For Royal Ballet; in his repertory ever since with several companies
GRAND PAS CLASSIQUE	Victor Gsovsky Daniel-François Auber	One performance only, with Yvette Chauviré at gala by the Stuttgart Ballet

Ballet and role	Choreographer and composer	Notes
*New solo in SWAN LAKE Prince Siegfreid	Nureyev Tchaikovsky	Introduced into Act 1 of Royal Ballet production

1962–63

† PRINCE IGOR Polovtsian Warrior	Fokine, revised by Ruth Page and Enrique Martinez Alexander Borodin	Four performances only with the Chicago Opera and Chicago Opera Ballet
THE MERRY WIDOW Danilo	Page Franz Lehar	One-act danced version with the Chicago Opera Ballet; this season only
THEME AND VARIATIONS	George Balanchine Tchaikovsky	With the American Ballet Theatre in Chicago; this season only
LA FILLE MAL GARDÉE Colin	Bronislava Nijinska, after Mikhail Mordkin Hertel	With the American Ballet Theatre in Chicago; this season only. See also under 1961–62 and 1973–74
ANTIGONE Etiocles	John Cranko Mikis Theodorakis	With the Royal Ballet; this season only
DIVERSIONS	Kenneth MacMillan Arthur Bliss	With the Royal Ballet; this season only
*MARGUERITE AND ARMAND Armand	Ashton Franz Liszt	With the Royal Ballet; also given later with other companies. In his repertory ever since

231

Ballet and role	Choreographer and composer	Notes
SYMPHONIC VARIATIONS	Ashton César Franck	With the Royal Ballet, one performance only

1963–64

Duet from LA SYLPHIDE James	Bournonville Herman Løvenskjold	On concert tour with Margot Fonteyn, then at RAD gala and other occasional performances. See also under 1964–65
PETRUSHKA Petrushka	Fokine Igor Stravinsky	With the Royal Ballet. Resumed the role several seasons later with Dutch National Ballet; in his repertory since then with various companies
†Kingdom of Shades from LA BAYADÈRE Solor	Petipa, revised by Nureyev Minkus	With the Royal Ballet; in his repertory ever since (also with Paris Opéra Ballet)
*FANTASIA IN C MINOR	MacMillan Bach	One performance only at RAD gala
†Pas de six from LAURENCIA	Chabukiani, staged by Nureyev Krein	For *Golden Hour* TV program and later at Royal Ballet gala and on U.S. tour
SWAN LAKE Prince Siegfried	After Petipa and Ivanov; some new choreography by Ashton and Nureyev Tchaikovsky	With the Royal Ballet; this version in repertory for nine seasons

232

Ballet and role	Choreograpner and composer	Notes
*IMAGES OF LOVE "Two Loves I Have"	MacMillan Peter Tranchell	With the Royal Ballet, this season only
HAMLET Hamlet	Robert Helpmann Tchaikovsky	With the Royal Ballet, also later with the Australian Ballet
*DIVERTIMENTO	MacMillan Béla Bartók	For gala by Western Theatre Ballet; this night only
SWAN LAKE Prince Siegfried	Cranko, after Petipa and Ivanov Tchaikovsky	With the Stuttgart Ballet
*RAYMONDA Jean de Brienne	Nureyev, after Petipa Glazunov	With the Royal Ballet; later mounted revised versions elsewhere and one-act version for Royal Ballet. In his repertory ever since

1964–65

*SWAN LAKE Prince Siegfried	Nureyev, after Petipa and Ivanov Tchaikovsky	With the Ballet of the Vienna State Opera; continuing in repertory
†Grand pas from PAQUITA	Nureyev, after Petipa Minkus	One performance only at RAD gala
LA SYLPHIDE James	Bournonville Løvenskjold	With National Ballet of Canada; in his repertory ever since with several companies

233

Ballet and role	Choreographer and composer	Notes
*ROMEO AND JULIET Romeo	MacMillan Sergei Prokofiev	With the Royal Ballet; in his repertory ever since
†Polovtsian dances from PRINCE IGOR Polovtsian Warrior	Fokine Borodin	With the Royal Ballet this season only
1965–66		
*TANCREDI \Tancredi	Nureyev Hans Werner Henze	With the Ballet of the Vienna State Opera, this season only
SONG OF THE EARTH Messenger of Death	MacMillan Gustav Mahler	With the Royal Ballet, initially this season only but resumed role in 1974–75
1966–67		
*THE SLEEPING BEAUTY Prince Florimund	Nureyev, after Petipa Tchaikovsky	With Ballet of La Scala, Milan; in his repertory ever since with this company, the National Ballet of Canada and London Festival Ballet
*DON QUIXOTE Basilio	Nureyev, after Petipa Minkus and others, arranged by John Lanchbery	With Ballet of the Vienna State Opera; in his repertory ever since with this and revised productions for the Australian Ballet and Marseilles Ballet

Ballet and role	Choreographer and composer	Notes
*PARADISE LOST The Man	Roland Petit Marius Constant	With the Royal Ballet; also the following season with Paris Opéra Ballet
LE JEUNE HOMME ET LA MORT The Young Man	Petit Bach	For French TV; this performance only

1967–68

†APOLLO Apollo	Balanchine Stravinsky	With Ballet of the Vienna State Opera; in his repertory ever since with several companies
THE NUTCRACKER Drosselmeyer and The Prince	Nureyev (Prince's solo in Act 2 by Vainonen) Tchaikovsky	With the Royal Swedish Ballet; in his repertory ever since with productions for Royal Ballet and at Milan and Buenos Aires
*JAZZ CALENDAR Friday's Child	Ashton Richard Rodney Bennett	With the Royal Ballet; some performances in later seasons
†BIRTHDAY OFFERING Leading man, including new solo	Ashton Glazunov	With the Royal Ballet, this season only
THE DREAM Oberon	Ashton Felix Mendelssohn-Bartholdy	With the Royal Ballet on European tour, initially, this season only but resumed role in 1975–76

Ballet and role	Choreographer and composer	Notes
1968–69		
*L' ESTASI Man	Petit Scriabin	With Ballet of La Scala, Milan, then with Paris Opéra Ballet; this season only
MONUMENT FOR A DEAD BOY The Boy	Rudi van Dantzig Jan Boerman	With Dutch National Ballet, this and next season
*PELLEAS AND MELISANDE Pelleas	Petit Arnold Schoenberg	With the Royal Ballet, this season only
New solo and duet in THE SLEEPING BEAUTY Prince Florimund	Ashton Tchaikovsky	With the Royal Ballet, in repertory for five seasons
1969–70		
SWAN LAKE Prince Siegfried	Vladimir Bourmeister, after Petipa and Ivanov Tchaikovsky	With the Paris Opéra Ballet (and in later seasons)
*THE ROPES OF TIME The Traveler	Van Dantzig Boerman	With the Royal Ballet and Dutch National Ballet, this season only
LES RENDEZVOUS	Ashton Auber	All except finale at Ashton farewell gala; complete work in his repertory with the Royal Ballet since then

236

Ballet and role	Choreographer and composer	Notes
Ballroom scene from APPARITIONS The Poet	Ashton Liszt	At Ashton farewell gala only
1970–71		
†DANCES AT A GATHERING	Jerome Robbins Chopin	With the Royal Ballet, in his continuing repertory
*BIG BERTHA	Paul Taylor Mechanical organ music	For American TV; specially adapted version of work later given by Taylor's company
*LIEDER EINES FAHRENDEN GESELLEN	Maurice Béjart Mahler	With Ballet of the Twentieth Century this season only; a few later performances elsewhere
LE SACRE DU PRINTEMPS The Chosen Youth	Béjart Stravinsky	With Ballet of the Twentieth Century, this season only
1971–72		
FIELD FIGURES	Glen Tetley Karlheinz Stockhausen	With Royal Ballet
CHECKMATE The First Red Knight	Ninette de Valois Bliss	With the Royal Ballet, this season only

237

Ballet and role	Choreographer and composer	Notes
AFTERNOON OF A FAUN	Robbins Claude Debussy	With the Royal Ballet; in his continuing repertory (also later with Paris Opéra Ballet)
AUREOLE	Taylor George Frideric Handel	With Paul Taylor Dance Company; in his continuing repertory with this and other companies
BOOK OF BEASTS The Illuminations	Taylor Miscellaneous	With Paul Taylor Dance Company; some further performances the next season
*SIDESHOW	MacMillan Stravinsky	With the Royal Ballet
*LABORINTUS	Tetley Luciano Berio	With the Royal Ballet

1972–73

†THE MOOR'S PAVANE The Moor	José Limón Henry Purcell	With National Ballet of Canada; in his continuing repertory with this and other companies
SWAN LAKE Prince Siegfried	Bruhn, after Petipa and Ivanov Tchaikovsky	With National Ballet of Canada

Ballet and role	Choreographer and composer	Notes
†PRODIGAL SON The Prodigal	Balanchine Prokofiev	With the Royal Ballet; in his continuing repertory with this company and Paris Opéra Ballet

1973–74

Ballet and role	Choreographer and composer	Notes
AGON First pas de trois	Balanchine Stravinsky	With the Royal Ballet; in his continuing repertory with this company and Paris Opéra Ballet
†DON JUAN Don Juan	John Neumeier Christoph Willibald Gluck and Tomás Luis de Victoria	With the National Ballet of Canada
MANON Des Grieux	MacMillan Jules Massenet	With the Royal Ballet
LA FILLE MAL GARDÉE Colas	Ashton Louis-Joseph-Ferdinand Herold, arranged by Lanchbery	With the Royal Ballet

1974–75

Ballet and role	Choreographer and composer	Notes
*TRISTAN Tristan	Tetley Henze	With the Paris Opéra Ballet
COPPELIA Franz	Bruhn Léo Delibes	With the National Ballet of Canada

Ballet and role	Choreographer and composer	Notes
*LUCIFER Lucifer	Martha Graham Halim El-Dabh	Initially at fund-raising gala by Martha Graham Dance Company

Nureyev's Productions

THE NUTCRACKER

Ballet in two acts after the story *Nussknacker und Mausekönig*
by E. T. A. Hoffmann
Music by Piotr Ilyich Tchaikovsky

Pas de deux from Act 2 (choreography by Nureyev after Vassili
Vainonen, man's solo by Vainonen) for himself and Rosella Hightower. First performance at Cannes, January 6, 1962.

Complete ballet (choreography and production by Nureyev, ex-
cept the Prince's solo in Act 2 by Vainonen) for the Royal Swedish
Ballet. Scenery by Renzo Mongiardino, costumes by Claude Gas-
tine and Rostislav Doboujinsky. First given at the Royal Theater,
Stockholm, November 17, 1967, with Mariane Orlando as Clara,
Caj Selling as Drosselmeyer and the Prince.

Complete ballet for the Royal Ballet. Choreography and production considerably revised from the Stockholm production. Scenery and costumes by Nicholas Georgiadis. First given at the Royal
Opera House, Covent Garden, February 29, 1968, with Merle Park
as Clara, Nureyev as Drosselmeyer and the Prince. (The pas de
deux from this production later danced by Nureyev with various
partners as a separate number during guest appearances with several other companies.)

241

Complete ballet for Ballet of La Scala, Milan. Some revision of Nureyev's staging and Georgiadis' designs. First given at Teatro alla Scala, September 18, 1969, with Liliana Cosi as Clara and Nureyev as Drosselmeyer and the Prince.

Complete ballet for Ballet of Teatro Colón, Buenos Aires. Further revision of production (Nureyev) and designs (Georgiadis). First given on April 6, 1971.

Revival of the complete ballet for the Royal Ballet with further revisions by Nureyev and Georgiadis. First given at the Royal Opera House, Covent Garden, December 3, 1973, with Park and Nureyev.

RAYMONDA

Ballet in three acts. Original story by Lydia Pashkova and Marius Petipa
Music by Alexander Glazunov

Pas de quatre (choreography by Nureyev after Petipa) for concert performances by Sonia Arova, Rosella Hightower, Erik Bruhn and Nureyev. First performance at Cannes, January 6, 1962.

Dances from Act 3 (choreography by Nureyev after Petipa) for concert tour by group headed by Margot Fonteyn and Nureyev, summer, 1963.

Complete ballet (choreography by Nureyev after Petipa, adaptation and production by Nureyev, music edited by Ashley Lawrence) for the Royal Ballet's smaller company. Scenery and costumes by Beni Montresor. First performance at the Teatro Nuovo, Spoleto, June 19, 1964, with Doreen Wells as Raymonda and Nureyev as Jean de Brienne.

Complete ballet (choreography and new production by Nureyev after Petipa) for the Australian Ballet. Scenery by Ralph Koltai, costumes by Nadine Baylis. First performance at the Birmingham

242

Theater, November 6, 1965, with Margot Fonteyn as Raymonda and Nureyev as Jean de Brienne.

Act 3 (choreography by Nureyev after Petipa) in a new production for the Royal Ballet's smaller company. Scenery and costumes by Barry Kay. First performance at the Opera House, Helsinki, May 7, 1966, with Fonteyn and Keith Rosson.

Act 3 (choreography by Nureyev after Petipa) for the Norwegian Ballet. Scenery by Koltai, costumes by Baylis. First performance at the Opera House, Oslo, January 16, 1968, with Inger Johanne Rütter and Thor Sutowsky.

Act 3 in an expanded version with some solos from other acts (choreography by Nureyev after Petipa) for the Royal Ballet's larger company. Scenery and costumes by Barry Kay. First performance at the Royal Opera House, Covent Garden, March 27, 1969, with Svetlana Beriosova and Donald MacLeary.

Complete ballet (entirely revised production and choreography by Nureyev after Petipa) for the Ballet of the Zurich Opera House. Scenery and costumes by Nicholas Georgiadis. First performance, January 22, 1972, with Marcia Haydée and Nureyev.

Complete ballet (choreography by Nureyev after Petipa) for American Ballet Theatre. Scenery and costumes by Georgiadis. First performance at Jones Hall, Houston, June 26, 1975, with Cynthia Gregory and Nureyev.

THE SLEEPING BEAUTY

Ballet in four acts. Original story by Marius Petipa and Ivan Vsevolozhsky after the fairy tale by Charles Perrault
Music by Piotr Tchaikovsky

New solo for Prince Florimund in Act 3 (choreography traditional in the Kirov Ballet, revived by Nureyev) for the Royal Ballet's production. First performance at the Royal Opera House, Covent Garden, April 21, 1962, by Donald MacLeary.

NUREYEV

Complete ballet (choreography and production by Nureyev after Petipa) for the Ballet of La Scala, Milan. Scenery and costumes by Nicholas Georgiadis. First performance at Teatro alla Scala, September 22, 1966, with Carla Fracci as Princess Aurora and Nureyev as Prince Florimund.

Complete ballet for the National Ballet of Canada. Scenery and costumes by Georgiadis. First performance at the National Arts Centre, Ottawa, September 1, 1972, with Veronica Tennant as Princess Aurora and Nureyev as Prince Florimund.

Complete ballet for London Festival Ballet. Scenery and costumes by Geordiadis. First performance at the London Coliseum, April 16, 1975, with Eva Evdokimova as Princess Aurora and Nureyev as Prince Florimund.

SWAN LAKE

Ballet in four acts. Original story by V. P. Begichev and Vassili Geltzer
Music by Piotr Tchaikovsky

New solo (choreography by Nureyev) for Prince Siegfried in Act 1 of the Royal Ballet's production. First performance at the Royal Opera House, Covent Garden, June 22, 1962, by Nureyev.

Polonaise and mazurka in new production by the Royal Ballet. Choreography by Nureyev. First performance at the Royal Opera House, Covent Garden, December 12, 1963.

Complete ballet (choreography and production by Nureyev after Petipa and Ivanov) for the Ballet of the Vienna State Opera. Scenery and costumes by Nicholas Georgiadis. First performance, October 15, 1964, with Margot Fonteyn as Odette and Odile, Nureyev as Prince Siegfried.

THE CORSAIR

Pas de deux, taken from a ballet in three acts with original book by Vernoy de Saint-Georges and Joseph Mazilier after Byron's

poem; original choreography by Mazilier later revived, amended and supplemented by Marius Petipa
Music originally by Adolphe Adam; additional music by Drigo, Minkus and Pugni

This pas de deux (which was at first a pas de trois) was one of Petipa's additions; the music is by Riccardo Drigo and Ludwig Minkus. The choreography for the man's solo was a revision by Vakhtang Chabukiani.

Pas de deux (choreography by Nureyev after Petipa) for Bell Telephone television program, New York, September, 1962. Performed by Lupe Serrano and Nureyev. Later included in repertory of the American Ballet Theatre with this cast.

Pas de deux for gala performance by the Chicago Opera Ballet, October, 1962. Performed by Sonia Arova and Nureyev.

Pas de deux for the Royal Ballet. Woman's costume by André Levasseur, man's costume by Nureyev. First performance at the Royal Opera House, Covent Garden, November 3, 1962, with Margot Fonteyn and Nureyev.

GAYANE

Pas de deux, taken from a ballet in four acts with original story by Konstantin Derzhavin, produced in several different versions with choreography by Nina Anisimova
Music by Aram Khachaturian

Pas de deux (choreography by Nina Anisimova, revived by Nureyev) for RAD gala, Theatre Royal, Drury Lane, December 6, 1962. Danced by Margot Fonteyn and Viktor Rona. Subsequently in Fonteyn's concert repertory with various partners, including Nureyev.

DIANA AND ACTEON

Pas de deux taken from *Esmeralda,* a ballet in three acts with

245

original story and choreography by Jules Perrot
Music by Cesare Pugni

This pas de deux comes from the production by Agrippina Vaganova in 1935 with new choreography for the man's solo by Vakhtang Chabukiani.

Pas de deux revived by Nureyev for Bell Telephone television program in New York, filmed July, 1963. Costumes by Nureyev. Danced by Svetlana Beriosova and Nureyev, who performed it also at RAD gala, Theatre Royal, Drury Lane, December 5, 1963.

Pas de deux revived by Nureyev for the American Ballet Theatre. First performance at the New York State Theater, July 3, 1973, with Eleanor D'Antuono and Ted Kivitt.

LA BAYADÈRE

Act 4 (the Kingdom of Shades) from a ballet in five acts with original story by Sergei Khudekov and Marius Petipa after a play by Kalidasa. Choreography by Petipa. Choreography for Solor's solo by Vakhtang Chabukiani (originally for the grand pas in Act 2)
Music by Ludwig Minkus

Complete version of the Kingdom of Shades (choreography by Petipa and Chabukiani, revised by Nureyev) for the Royal Ballet. Costumes by Philip Prowse. First performance at the Royal Opera House, Covent Garden, November 27, 1963, with Margot Fonteyn as Nikiya and Nureyev as Solor.

Complete version of the Kingdom of Shades for the Ballet of the Paris Opéra. Costumes by Martin Kamer. First performance at the Théâtre National de l'Opéra, October 10, 1974, with Noëlla Pontois as Nikiya and Nureyev as Solor.

PAQUITA

Grand pas from a ballet in two acts with original book by Paul Foucher and Joseph Mazilier, choreography by Mazilier, later revised by Marius Petipa

Music for the original ballet by Edward Deldevez; additional music (including most of this grand pas) by Ludwig Minkus

Grand pas (choreography by Petipa, revived by Nureyev) for RAD gala, Theatre Royal, Drury Lane, November 17, 1964. Costumes by Philip Prowse. Danced by Margot Fonteyn, Nureyev and dancers of the Royal Ballet and the Royal Ballet School.

This production later revived for performances organized by Marika Besobrazova in Monte Carlo and subsequently staged by her for the Ballet of La Scala, Milan (March 13, 1970, costumes by Enrico d'Assia), dancers of the Vienna State Opera at Salzburg (June 20, 1971) and the American Ballet Theatre (July 6, 1971).

LAURENCIA

Pas de six from a ballet in three acts with original story by Yevgeny Mandelberg after Lope de Vega's play *Fuente Ovejuna*. Choreography by Vakhtang Chabukiani
Music by Alexander Krein

Pas de six (choreography by Chabukiani, revived by Nureyev) for the Royal Ballet; first performed on *Golden Hour* television program broadcast from the Royal Opera House, Covent Garden, February 9, 1964, then at gala performance in the same theater, March 24, 1965. Danced by Nadia Nerina, Merle Park, Antoinette Sibley, Nureyev, Christopher Gable, Graham Usher.

This production revived for the Royal Ballet's touring company, April 26, 1972.

TANCREDI

Ballet in one act, with an original story by Peter Csobadi, adapted by Nureyev. Choreography by Nureyev. Scenery and costumes by Barry Kay
Music by Hans Werner Henze

Created for the Ballet of the Vienna State Opera. First perfor-

247

mance, May 18, 1966, with Nureyev as Tancredi, Lisl Maar as the First Female Image and Ully Wührer as the Second Female Image.

DON QUIXOTE

Ballet in three acts, with original book by Marius Petipa after the novel by Cervantes, adapted by Nureyev. Choreography originally by Petipa, later revised by Alexander Gorsky. New choreography and production by Nureyev after Petipa
Music by Ludwig Minkus with some later additions, arranged and orchestrated by John Lanchbery

Produced by Nureyev for the Ballet of the Vienna State Opera. Scenery and costumes by Barry Kay. First performance, December 1, 1966, with Ully Wührer as Kitri and Dulcinea, Nureyev as Basilio and Michael Birkmeyer as Don Quixote.

Produced by Nureyev in a new version for the Australian Ballet. First performance at Adelaide, March 28, 1970, with Lucette Aldous as Kitri and Dulcinea, Nureyev as Basilio and Robert Helpmann as Don Quixote.

Produced by Nureyev with some additional choreography for the Ballet of the Marseilles Opera House. First performance, November 4, 1971, with Aldous, Nureyev and Helpmann.

Revised production by Nureyev (incorporating his additional choreography from the Marseilles version) for the Australian Ballet. First performance at the Hordern Pavilion, Sydney, November 4, 1972, with Aldous, Nureyev and Helpmann. Filmed later that month.

Acknowledgments

AS WELL AS Nureyev himself, many other busy people put themselves out to help while I was writing this book. I want to thank especially all those dancers, choreographers and other colleagues of Nureyev who allowed me to quote their opinions of him. I owe special gratitude to Erik Bruhn and Rudi van Dantzig, since they were responsible for my first getting to know Nureyev offstage.

Many friends and acquaintances provided valuable background information. Maude Lloyd and Nigel Gosling, in particular, whose own writings about Nureyev have always shown illuminating insight, allowed me to quote from early descriptions of him at work. Oleg Kerensky kindly read the typescript and made helpful suggestions. Anne Borg, Bertil Hagman, Rosella Hightower, Björn Holmgren, Alfred Oberzaucher and David Palmer helped track down facts and pictures from various countries. Moira McCaffery kindly lent her drawings of Nureyev. Beverley Gallegos and Elaine Rawlings lent photographs from their private collections, and Peter Moldon, responsible for editing the illustrations, showed an interest beyond the call of duty.

The managements of many theaters have made it possible for me to watch Nureyev's performances with various companies, and the Royal Ballet generously allowed me to travel to Israel with the company and to watch rehearsals there and in London. Iris Law, secretary to successive directors of the Royal Ballet, was notably helpful in getting hold of people for me. I am grateful to all these and also to the dancers who allowed themselves to be observed in the unflattering circumstances of class or rehearsal.

Finally, I am happy to be able to acknowledge the help, suggestions and encouragement of my wife, Judith. Without her participation, this book would have been less enjoyable to write and less interesting to read.

Index

Index of Names

251

Index of Ballets